The Blessed Family

The Blessed Family

Matthew E. Bullen

iUniverse, Inc.

New York Lincoln Shanghai

The Blessed Family

Copyright © 2005 by Matthew E. Bullen

iUniverse books may be ordered through booksellers or by contacting:

iUniverse
2021 Pine Lake Road, Suite 100
Lincoln, NE 68512
www.iuniverse.com
1-800-Authors (1-800-288-4677)

ISBN-13: 978-0-595-37121-1 (pbk)
ISBN-13: 978-0-595-81520-3 (ebk)
ISBN-10: 0-595-37121-3 (pbk)
ISBN-10: 0-595-81520-0 (ebk)

Printed in the United States of America

To our precious Lord and Savior Jesus Christ, whose Word is true, relevant, and sufficient. And to all of the wonderful families, mentors, and ministries who have poured their wisdom into our family over the years. We dedicate this work.

Contents

Foreword

He was 52 years old, and on top of the world. At least that's what he wanted me to think as we made small talk before the flight. He was a very successful businessman who had just put off his family vacation because his company needed him in South America on short notice. As we talked, I discovered that he traveled 45 weeks a year (Monday thru Friday), and hadn't been home in two weeks.

As he told me about his house on the golf course, his upscale, suburban life complete with a wife and three daughters, I could no longer contain myself. I looked him straight in his eyes and asked, "How is your marriage?" He paused, apparently stunned at my question, and then replied, "It's been better." Sensing that he was open to discussing the issue further, I asked, "How is your relationship with your daughters?" "Hot and cold," he replied, handing his empty cup to the flight attendant.

As the conversation went on, I told this man that he was free to tell me at any time that I was getting too personal. He simply smiled, shook his head, and said, "I need somebody in my life that is willing to say these things." As it turns out, this man's marriage was a shambles; his daughters were out of control, and all he could think about was putting in 5 more years so he could retire on easy street. What's worse, this man claimed to be a Christian, and was a member in good standing at his local church (although he knew virtually nothing of the gospel). I couldn't help thinking, "I wish this guy could meet my friend Matt Bullen."

It is encounters like this (that happen far too often) that give me a sense of urgency about the current state of the family in our culture. This man's story is only exceptional in the level of financial success he has acquired. His lack of understanding in the areas of marriage, family, child training and discipleship has unfortunately become the norm even among Christians. That is why we need books like *The Blessed Family*. The Bullens are the first to admit that they are not perfect. However, anyone who has spent five minutes in their home knows that these people get it, and they need to give it away.

How can a man live in a house with five teenagers and have harmony? How can a family living in today's culture afford to homeschool five children? How can they even afford for mom to stay at home? Quite simply, they must be committed to living according to the simple, straightforward instructions found in

xii The Blessed Family

the Word of God. *The Blessed Family* is a classic example of the proverbial beggar telling other beggars where he found bread.

As you read the following pages, I want you to know that these people are near and dear to my heart, and that I have seen the principles in these pages lived out before my very eyes. Matt and Lisa Bullen are like a couple of scientists who have found the cure for Cancer. As they looked around at a world full of sick families, they wanted to share their cure with others. Primarily, they wanted to tell the next ten generations of Bullens how it all started.

What would happen if you took the book of Proverbs seriously and applied it to the way you raised your children, loved your wife, organized your house, and impacted the world? Read *The Blessed Family* and you'll find out.

Dr. Voddie T. Baucham Jr.
Author and Bible Teacher

Preface

Over the years, many people have come to us wondering what the secret is to our joyful, peaceful, and happy family. When people ask that question, the Lord often gives us the opportunity to counsel, instruct, and share from God's Word the principles that he has been teaching us these twenty years. We also are able to direct them to the mentors, materials, and ministries that have been invaluable in our own growth as a Christian family. Many of those who have come to us for advice have asked that we put down in writing what the Lord has taught us regarding family. This book is a humble attempt to put into words our vision for a blessed family and how to have one.

We do make a couple of assumptions about the readers here. We assume them to be Christians who have the Holy Spirit to guide and direct them in all truth, and we assume that they have a basic knowledge of the Bible. Some of what is written in these pages could easily be misunderstood or misapplied if an individual does not have the Holy Spirit's wisdom to guide them. We have not tried to create a reference work on the family or a theological thesis on marriage, parenting, or life. There are many of those fine works already in existence. We are not experts, scholars, or theologians. We are merely a family who loves God and his Word. We have simply tried to share the truths about raising a godly family that are near and dear to our heart.

The chapters that follow are not exhaustive works on the particular subjects that they cover; they are simply meant to whet the appetite and inspire the reader to study beyond this book.

The works of many authors and speakers have contributed to our family's worldview through their books, tapes, videos, and magazine articles. Undoubtedly much of their teachings are interwoven throughout this book, and we have tried to give credit where appropriate.

On the day God impressed on Matthew to write this book, he came home and gathered the family around him. He told us of his vision and asked us to start thinking about what we felt made a blessed family. In about two hours, we had compiled a list of topics that eventually became the table of contents for this book. We were all amazed at how quickly and easily the list of topics came together. We knew that God was moving us to pull together the things that he has taught us about shaping a Christian family in a form that we could share with others. Most of these truths we learned out of our failures. Building a godly family requires patient endurance. We must trust in the Lord to take our fallible efforts and, by his grace, cause them to bring forth good fruit unto his glory. It is our prayer that future generations of the Bullen family and all those who read these pages will be encouraged and inspired to build a family that brings glory to God.

The Bullen Family,
Matthew, Lisa, Luke (19), Levi (18), Rebekah (16), Beverly (14), and Brooke (12)
June 2005

All scripture quotations are taken from the King James Bible.

Visit our website at www.theblessedfamily.com

The Value of a Vision

✦

Psalm 128:1–4

Blessed is every one that feareth the LORD; that walketh in his ways. For thou shalt eat the labour of thine hands: happy shalt thou be and it shall be well with thee. Thy wife shall be as a fruitful vine by the sides of thine house: thy children like olive plants round about thy table. Behold, that thus shall the man be blessed that feareth the LORD.

What is a blessed family? What does one look like, act like, and sound like? In the pages of this book, we will lay out for you from the scriptures our vision of a blessed family and the essential truths that make it so. In the verse above, we see a glimpse of King David's vision for the family. God's ultimate vision for each member of his family, and consequently for each member of our families, is to become like Jesus: *"For whom he did foreknow, he also did predestinate to be conformed to the image of his Son, that he might be the firstborn among many brethren."*

One thing is certain: in building a family that brings glory to God and brings joy and rest to our souls, we must first and foremost crystallize in our heart a clear vision of what we desire our family to be like and then set out by faith to achieve that ideal.

As in every endeavor of life, before beginning the pursuit of a goal, the desired end should be defined. No archer could judge the quality of his aim without a target at which to shoot. Likewise, if a father and mother have not established a picture in their hearts and minds of what the finished product will be, there is no chance of ever attaining the desired end.

Imagine a family where the father is the spiritual leader of his home, where the wife joyously serves her family, and where the children sweetly obey and are kind to each other. Envision young men who are respectful, responsible, and kind. Picture young women who are loving and gentle, yet resolute and bold in their faith.

1

Visualize a home where there is singing, laughter, and harmony and where encouragement dwells. And when anyone enters this haven, they are immediately struck by the peace and joy that reside therein. Think about a husband and wife who cherish each other and who build each other up in the eyes of their children. Fancy a father who is the hero of his sons and the delight of his daughters. Picture a mother who is refreshed by her children and is renewed by her husband. She is the most happy when enjoying the presence of her family.

Can we see a father who consistently instructs his family in the things of God, children who love the Bible and have hearts for Christ? Do we dare to look down through the generations and see an unbroken line of faithfulness in our children and our children's children? Can we perceive of a family who prefer to be with each other as opposed to being apart? Do we see little ones who sit quietly in church and are happy and contented, children who are willing to serve and never complain? We dream of being a family who changes the world one family at a time and one generation at a time.

Maybe your vision is not so lofty at this point. Maybe you would just like for your children to obey the first time…or even at all. Each vision will be diverse and unique as the family itself. Whatever our vision, we can know that God is faithful and his Word is true, and what he has promised he will perform as we obey in faith the truths of scripture.

A family like this does not happen by accident. It is not that some families are luckier than others or that some children just have the right temperament to be kind and obedient and serving. Blessed families are built, shaped, and formed by diligent effort. First, we must get a vision of what our home can be and what the scripture says it should be. As the God-ordained leader of their families, it is the fathers' duty to establish the vision in their families and to keep it ever before their eyes. They should go to the Lord and get a vision of what he wants their families to be and to do for his kingdom and then take the lead. Their families will be glad to follow once they see they are sincere.

Early on in my marriage to my wife, the two of us began the habit of going to dinner once a week and talking about our vision. We would share our hearts with each other and dream about how things might be in our future. We would write down our financial, educational, and spiritual goals for our family. We would search the scriptures and discuss what we found regarding God's blessing upon families. This brought strength and unity to our marriage and kept us focused on our purpose of raising a godly family. Years later we have been able to look back and realize that everything that God has allowed us to accomplish in our marriage, family, finances, and ministry we first discussed and wrote down in one of those dinner dream-building sessions.

Our ultimate vision involves the future generations of the Bullen family. The potential results of training our children to love God, love others, and eventually train their own children to do so are staggering. We have five children. For the sake of illustration, we will assume that each of our children will marry and have five children and that each of those children will marry and have five children and so on. In just five generations (possibly still within our lifetime) there will be over six thousand souls being influenced by our training today. In ten generations, the number is twenty million souls. In three more generations, it is a billion souls. Can there be anything more important than the discipleship of our children? This should drive us to our knees to seek a vision and a passion from the Lord for the kingdom work we must do in our home. Have you ever wished that you could change the world? The future of the world lives in your home.

Is it far-fetched to think that we could make a difference or even be remembered twelve or thirteen generations from now? The name Bullen is Norman and comes from the city of Boulogne, France. The first Bullen in England was Sir Richard Bullen, the grandson of Count Eustace de Boulogne, who rode with William the Conqueror at the Battle of Hastings in AD 1066. The first Bullen in America, our ancestor, was Samuel Bullen, who arrived on the Speedwell in Dedham, Massachusetts, in 1634, only fourteen years after the Pilgrims landed at Plymouth. He was a deacon and by all accounts a godly man. He was a signer of the Dedham Compact. There are thirteen generations between him and us, and we know the names of every man and woman. So it is reasonable to assume that we could leave a godly heritage that extends to twelve or thirteen generations.

We love the story of William and Catherine Booth, the founders of the Salvation Army. They loved God and loved others. They had eight children who, when they were grown, went all over the world preaching the gospel of Jesus. Those eight children had forty-five children who grew up in homes where their parents loved God and loved others. Every one of those forty-five grandchildren, when they were grown, followed the faith of their parents and scattered throughout the world preaching the gospel. To this day, there are great-grandchildren of William and Catherine Booth preaching the gospel around the globe.

Study the godly heritage of Christian greats such as Hudson Taylor. He was a third-generation preacher of the gospel whom God sent to China. There is a nine-generation unbroken lineage of godly men in the Taylor family, and one of them is a missionary in Thailand today. Study the godly heritage that God gave to Jonathan Edwards and his wife. They had ten children whom they raised for

God. The state of New York did a study on the five generations of the Edwards family. From their 729 descendants studied, 300 became preachers, 65 became college professors, 13 became university presidents, 60 became authors, 3 were congressmen, and 1 was a vice president of the United States. God is no respecter of persons. What he has done for others, he can do for us. Praise be to God!

Get a vision! Countless future generations and perhaps the future of Christendom depends on it. Write it down, pray over it, and resolve to have it no matter what the cost!

Psalms 71:18: Now also when I am old and grayheaded, O God, forsake me not; until I have shewed thy strength unto this generation, and thy power to every one that is to come.

Deuteronomy 4:9: Only take heed to thyself, and keep thy soul diligently, lest thou forget the things which thine eyes have seen, and lest they depart from thy heart all the days of thy life: but teach them thy sons, and thy sons' sons;

The Foundation of Faith

✦

Luke 6:47–48
Whosoever cometh to me and heareth my sayings and doeth them, I will shew you to whom he is like: He is like a man which built an house and digged deep and laid the foundation on a rock: and when the flood arose, the stream beat vehemently upon that house and could not shake it: for it was founded upon a rock.

In setting out to construct a godly family, we must first examine the foundation upon which we are attempting to build. When the floods of a godless culture begin to crash against our family, will it stand or will it fall?

Jesus said that building on a solid foundation requires hearing his sayings (God's word) and then doing them (faith). The most direct and understandable definition of faith that we have ever come across is this: *faith is taking God at his Word.* It is, first of all, knowing his Word and second, accepting, resting in, trusting, and acting upon the truths contained therein.

Hebrews 11:6: *But without faith it is impossible to please him: for he that cometh to God must believe that he is and that he is a rewarder of them that diligently seek him.*

We must settle forever in our minds that God says what he means and means what he says. Every Word of God is true, whether or not we can always understand or explain it. God's Word is true even if it flies in the face of current popular cultural ideas. It is true even if it is diametrically opposed to what the social "experts" of the day are touting. If we are to succeed in fashioning a family that glorifies God, we must have a rock-solid basis from which to start, and that basis is the Holy Bible. If we are to have the blessedness that is promised in his Word, then we must accept the sufficiency of his Word to teach us how to receive it. No amount of psychology or philosophy, whether "Christian" or otherwise, can bring the results we seek because only the Bible has the supernatural power of the Almighty behind it.

1 Corinthians 2:5: That your faith should not stand in the wisdom of men, but in the power of God.

God's Word is adequate in every aspect. It is not outdated or antiquated. It is relevant as to its teaching, its examples, its means and methods, and its models. If we ever find ourselves disagreeing with its plain teachings, we can rest assured that we are wrong and God is right. There are many helpful books, tapes, and videos out there that can clarify and give practical examples of how to apply the principles of the Word, but they must never be substitutes for knowing and faithfully obeying the voice of God. Frankly, if all we had was the book of Proverbs, we could raise delightful children, have a happy marriage, and be successful in this world. The eternal, omniscient Creator of the universe put down in one book, the Bible, all that mankind would ever need to know in order to become all that God desires. We simply need to know it, believe it, and obey it.

Now, most Christians would claim to believe the Bible and would never dream of disagreeing with its teachings. Yet is it the first place we go to for answers? Do we really believe that it applies to *everything* in our lives? For instance, when the Bible says in Proverbs 22:15, *"Foolishness is bound in the heart of a child; but the rod of correction shall drive it far from him,"* do we administer the rod for foolishness or do we try "time-outs," "grounding," "counting to 10," or any number of other psychobabble, nonbiblical, "creative" methods of correction? Faith is more than giving lip service to the Word. It is obeying it consistently and without question. Of course, we will deal with biblical correction in another chapter, but this is a classic example of Christians believing the Word for most things and missing the boat on others.

Hebrews 11:1: Now faith is the substance of things hoped for, the evidence of things not seen.

Another aspect of faith is that it allows us to see what is not yet apparent. This goes back to our discussion of having a vision. Once we have established our vision for our family, it may take years of hard work before we fully realize that ideal. Although we will often see dramatic results almost immediately once we start applying the truths in this book, and although we will experience much blessedness along the way, faith ultimately works in the dark. If we walk by sight alone, we will quickly become discouraged and despair of ever attaining the reward. Faith is the evidence of things not seen. It is our proof that we have the victory even when no one else can see it yet. Faith is not an emotion. It is an act of our will to take God at his Word and rest in his wisdom and reliability whether we feel it with our emotions or not.

2 Corinthians 5:7: For we walk by faith, not by sight.

Many times we think of faith as a feeling or just really, really believing something. In reality, faith requires only that we believe that God is truthful and trustworthy, and then we can step out in complete confidence and obey his Word whether we feel like it or whether we can see the next step.

It takes faith for a man to go against his selfishness and laziness and become the priest of his home. It takes faith for a woman to trust God and submit to her husband and become his helpmeet. It takes faith to go against the culture and rear our children according to the scriptures. It takes faith for a teenager to renounce the foolish youth culture of his day and stand forth as a godly example to the young people within his circle of influence.

If we are to benefit from the incredible promises God has made in his Word to families, it is imperative that we obey, by faith, the commands and teachings in his Word that are directed to families.

In this age of computers, it is easier than ever to study God's word. We use a free software program called e-Sword (www.e-sword.net). We can quickly do a study of every place in the Bible a certain word or phrase is used. We enjoy word studies on a variety of topics such as correction, instruction, foolishness, marriage, fathers, mothers, generation, seed, rod, sons, daughters, blessing, house, families, home, love, delight, and so on. Find out what God thinks on any number of subjects related to the family, and then start applying them in your home and watch the Holy Spirit do his work! You don't have to be a theologian to know what God wants from you. Simply look at what he says over and over again on a certain subject, and you will really begin to understand what he desires.

Jeremiah 29:13: And ye shall seek me and find me, when ye shall search for me with all your heart.

The Pursuit of Priorities

✦

Matthew 6:33
But seek ye first the kingdom of God and his righteousness; and all these things shall be added unto you.

It has been said that the reason we spend so much of our time on urgencies and so little of our time on priorities is that the urgencies shout and the priorities whisper.

If we are to have a blessed family, we must establish priorities in our lives that will allow us to stay focused on the eternal and not get distracted by the temporal.

As with so many of the topics in this book, we have learned these things from our failures rather than our successes. Thankfully, in Proverbs 24:16, we read, *"For a just man falleth seven times, and riseth up again: but the wicked shall fall into mischief."*

We are going to stumble, but God will lift us up and make us better for the experience.

Building a family that brings glory to God takes time. Since we are each given only twenty-four hours a day, it stands to reason that we should organize our time in such a way that we spend sufficient amounts of it on the things that are the most valuable to us. As with a vision, it is important that we clearly define what our priorities are and commit before God to give them the place of prominence that they deserve. Here is a list of priorities for you to consider:

I. God

Our first priority must be a personal and intimate relationship with our Lord. Abiding in his presence is the only place we will find the love, power, faith, joy, and so on that we need to be the person that God intended. His written Word is where we will find the truths we need to live our lives in a way that will bring glory to God. Spend time alone with him on a daily basis. Drink deeply of his grace and love, and when you come away, you will overflow onto those around you.

Psalm 42:1–2: *As the hart panteth after the water brooks, so panteth my soul after thee, O God. My soul thirsteth for God, for the living God: when shall I come and appear before God?*

II. Spouse

The premier relationship in our life, apart from God, must be with our spouse. God said, *"Therefore shall a man leave his father and his mother and shall cleave unto his wife: and they shall be one flesh"* (Genesis 2:24).

The Hebrew word here for *cleave* is *dabaq,* which is also translated in other passages as *keep, joined, stick, close, abide, pursued,* and so on. As we can see, God doesn't place this type of emphasis on any other relationship in our lives. We live in a society that finds it acceptable for a husband or wife to take a backseat to the outside, personal, and self-gratifying interest of the other. Such activities as career, recreation, children, sports, and yes, even ministry, become more important than a person's spouse. A blessed home demands a dad and mom who put each other ahead of every other person on the planet, period! If you had a world full of husbands and wives whose goal it was to out-love and out-serve the other, the divorce courts would have to close down and the juvenile detention centers would be boarded up!

Ephesians 5:33: *Nevertheless let every one of you in particular so love his wife even as himself; and the wife see that she reverence her husband.*

III. Children

Psalms 127:3–5
Lo, children are an heritage of the LORD: and the fruit of the womb is his reward. As arrows are in the hand of a mighty man; so are children of the youth. Happy is the man that hath his quiver full of them: they shall not be ashamed, but they shall speak with the enemies in the gate.

The greatest blessing God created on this earth, after our spouses, is our children. They are the only thing eternal that we will leave behind when we depart this earth. They are the hope of the future, the leaders of tomorrow, our heritage, and our namesake. Jobs can be replaced, possessions can be restored, money is fleeting, fame is fickle, health is fragile, youth quickly fades, pleasure is momentary, but godly offspring are everlasting! God has placed this incredible miracle called a child in our care and charge. We are commanded to teach, train, nurture, encourage, and set an example for this child. There is no greater calling than that of parent. Building godly men and women from infants is the most challenging, rewarding, frustrating, trying, stretching, magnificent occupation in the world.

Every other vocation in the world pales in comparison to the importance and grandeur of shaping eternal souls into soldiers of Christ. Satan knows this all too well and is an expert at diminishing this calling of parent and distracting us with multitudes of urgencies that cry out for our attention. He sees that Christianity is always one generation from extinction. God has no grandchildren. It is no wonder his biggest guns are aimed at our children. Entertainment, art, advertising, marketing, and propaganda of many forms are focused on the youth of our country because the world knows what many in God's kingdom have forgotten: if you capture the hearts and minds of the children, you own the future!

IV. Provision

1 Timothy 5:8: But if any provide not for his own and specially for those of his own house, he hath denied the faith and is worse than an infidel.
Proverbs 21:25: The desire of the slothful killeth him; for his hands refuse to labour.
Proverbs 22:29: Seest thou a man diligent in his business? he shall stand before kings; he shall not stand before mean men.

Early in our ministry we arrived at the idea that working was a sign of a lack of genuine faith. We believed that we should only witness for Christ and preach and that God would provide for us financially. The problem was that we were so legalistic about this that we despised in our hearts those who worked for a living. We were vainly proud of our commitment to "live by faith." God allowed us to suffer some serious privations before we finally realized that God honors and blesses hard work and by the grace of God amended our ways.

It is God's design that we labor for provision in this life. When Adam was created and placed in the garden, God first gave him the job of naming the animals and then later of tending the garden. Eve was given to Adam as his helper in this work. Men are created with an internal need to achieve and to be productive. They find most of their fulfillment in this life from their profession. Honest work is God's plan for providing for our families and is part of our responsibility as husbands and fathers. The danger is that so often men are tempted to put their work ahead of their families. We abdicate our God-given responsibility to love our wife and bring up our children in the nurture and admonition of the Lord. I wish we had a nickel for every time we've heard a man say, "My job has to come first because that is how I take care of my family." All provision comes from the Lord, so it only makes sense to pursue it his way, and his way is not to pursue it at the exclusion of our duties as husbands and fathers. Women are created with an internal need to help their husbands, and they find their greatest fulfillment when they are following their God-given "programming." The danger is that so often because the men in their lives are losing themselves in their work or losing themselves in their recreational activities, the woman despairs of keeping the home and raising the children by herself and goes out to find her fulfillment in the work world, hence the state of our nation today. Men, work to provide the funds to finance your vision and build your blessed family. Women, take God at his Word, by faith, and commit yourself to helping your man fulfill his God-given responsibilities on this earth.

V. Church and Ministry

The church is a great example of another wonderful priority that, if taken out of order, can be very damaging to a blessed family. Many times we are very tempted to believe that "God's work," that is, being actively involved in organized religion, is our number one priority. Loving and serving others is the responsibility of every Christian and it is a sweet calling, but it must never come before the family itself. We have had pastors tell us that the church and its programs should come before family and that the family should just try to understand. Of course, they lost their children to the world, the flesh, and the devil.

In our early marriage, we founded two nationwide evangelistic youth ministries, Teens Unlimited and later Save America Ministries. We threw ourselves into this work with reckless abandon. God blessed and hundreds of young people came to Christ during this season of our lives. However, as our children came along, we began to see that we would have to balance our youth ministry with the immensely important work of training and taking the time to disciple our children. God eventually moved us away from full-time ministry completely, and we were able to devote our whole energy to rearing children. It has often been said that Satan doesn't need to get us to quit on God as long as he can just keep us so busy "serving God" that we don't do the will of God. However, there is always the other end of the spectrum where people neglect the church and serving others and make their family an idol. This is why it is very important that we establish our priorities and then stick to them for dear life. Our family's destiny depends on it.

VI. Everything Else

If the world understood what a blessing it is and how joyous it is to have the first five priorities in order and how wonderful all the other priorities can be once the first five are in place, they would not be so tempted to neglect the others and put their own pleasures first. Self-indulgence, as we will talk about later, is the greatest enemy of true success and happiness. Our culture today is sold on the premise "my pleasure is first and foremost." They just don't know what they don't know.

The Author of Authority

✦

1 Corinthians 11:3
But I would have you know, that the head of every man is Christ; and the head of the woman is the man; and the head of Christ is God.

Ladies and gentlemen, God is the Author of Authority. We are probably all amazed by that because we have been taught that it is a bunch of patriarchal, male chauvinist, egomaniacal, authoritarian types who invented the idea of authority. 1 Corinthians 11:3, as well as many other portions of scripture, make it very clear that God is the ultimate authority and that there is a "chain of command" that he has ordained. In order for God's blessings to rest upon a family, this chain of command must be firmly established and followed in the home.

The chain of command that God has ordained in the home is in descending order—Christ, husband, wife, and children. Unfortunately, in our culture today it is nearly always the opposite. The children run the home, and the mother is their slave, racing around to fulfill their every wish and desire. The father is the detached, don't-bother-me provider, if he is even present in the home at all. Christ is a name evoked on Sunday or holidays if at all. Even in Christian families, this trend has to some degree become the norm. The ideologies of feminism, moral relativism, and an evolutionary view of child rearing (modern child psychology) have for the most part stripped parents of their right and responsibility to "rule" their own homes. The Bible has not changed, however, and we must seek out what God says on the subject if we are to have the blessedness promised.

A man who is submitted to Christ and who accepts and understands his duty to rule his home in love is an awesome force in the world. He is also a great blessing and comfort to the woman who accepts and understands her obligation to follow him in all things and rule her children well. They are both a great blessing to the children who understand and accept their role as trainees who are being lovingly and, yes, sometimes sternly corrected and instructed so that they may become all that God intends for them. The blessedness is derived from the knowledge and sense of security that comes from knowing that we are not alone and unprotected in this world.

Children are happier and more fulfilled when they know someone is in charge and taking care of things. Wives are more relaxed and at peace when they know that their husband is bearing the burdens of decision making, provision, and direction for the family. The husband can bear his burden of authority with joy and peace because he knows that Jesus has provided for his protection and security in decision making through the Word, prayer, and faithful men in the body of Christ who serve as wise counsel.

Genesis 3:16: *Unto the woman he said, I will greatly multiply thy sorrow and thy conception; in sorrow thou shalt bring forth children; and thy desire shall be to thy husband and he shall rule over thee.*

1 Timothy 3:4–5: *One that ruleth well his own house, having his children in subjection with all gravity; (For if a man know not how to rule his own house, how shall he take care of the church of God?)*

Ephesians 5:21–25: *Submitting yourselves one to another in the fear of God. Wives, submit yourselves unto your own husbands, as unto the Lord. For the husband is the head of the wife, even as Christ is the head of the church: and he is the saviour of the body. Therefore as the church is subject unto Christ, so let the wives be to their own husbands in every thing. Husbands, love your wives, even as Christ also loved the church and gave himself for it;*

Titus 2:3–5: *The aged women likewise, that they be in behaviour as becometh holiness, not false accusers, not given to much wine, teachers of good things; That they may teach the young women to be sober, to love their husbands, to love their children, To be discreet, chaste, keepers at home, good, obedient to their own husbands, that the word of God be not blasphemed.*

We will cover in more detail the role of husband and wife later in the book. For now, let's look at the issue of parental authority in the home.

Ephesians 6:1: *Children, obey your parents in the Lord: for this is right.*

Colossians 3:20: *Children, obey your parents in all things: for this is well pleasing unto the Lord.*

Matthew 15:4: *For God commanded, saying, Honour thy father and mother: and, He that curseth father or mother, let him die the death.*

Nine different times in the Bible, God commands children to honor their father and mother, with the penalty for failing to do so being death! Parent, God has placed you in charge of your children. Father, God Almighty has appointed you as benevolent ruler of your home. Mother, God has appointed you as royal under-ruler in your home. It is about time that parents stand up, step up, and take their place in the God-ordained chain of command and rule their homes in the fear of a Holy God!

We often joke in our home that the cause of the challenges that we observe with parents of unruly children in the world around us can be summed up in one word: spineless. We have jokingly remarked over the years that our children have two choices when told to do something by their parents. They can do it with a knot on their head or without a knot on their head—it is their choice! Though humorous, it does illustrate our seriousness about instant obedience. But sadly most parents have swallowed some part of the humanistic lie that authoritarianism is intrinsically evil and that no one has the right to force their beliefs, convictions, and rules on anyone else. Nonsense! It is our duty to establish rules and standards of behavior in our homes and then enforce them faithfully. Parents can and should be the final say in such things as where their children go, what they wear, who their friends are, what they eat, and how they behave without apology or guilt. Parents are God's emissaries on this earth to children, and we should not withdraw from acting as such. We have a direct command from God to bring up our children before the Lord, and he will hold us accountable for our stewardship of that duty.

How prevalent it is today to see parents whose children are disobedient, disrespectful, and outright rebellious. The parents act as if they are afraid to do anything about it for fear of inciting even more wrath from the miniature tyrants. They come to us wondering if this is normal and just part of raising children and if they should just get used to it. They are taken aback when we suggest that they should accept their divine commission to rule and begin to demand instant, unquestioning obedience and absolute respect from their children. We will discuss how to achieve this later, but we wish first to clearly lay out the fact that parents have an obligation before God to stand in his stead in their home and be "large and in charge."

It is a clear sign that we have not understood this concept if we allow our children to question our decisions and/or commands before first instantly obeying them. Another classic telltale sign is if we must tell them several times before they finally obey. In these cases the parent has not grasped that they are aiding and abetting their child in sinning against God! The parent is sinning as well because they are abdicating their responsibility to rule well their home.

Many parents are so desirous to have the acceptance and approval of their children that they are afraid to make a controversial decision or demand submission from them. Parents, get your acceptance and approval from each other and from

God and be the kind of confident, sincere, authoritative parent that your children can look up to and genuinely respect. Having your child's respect is much more valuable and gratifying than an endless search for the approval of a self-indulged child who sees you merely as a means of gratifying himself.

The Bullen children know that Dad is king and Mother is queen, and they are contented and at peace because they know that they are then princes and princesses and they are under the protection and benevolent rule of a dad and mom who love them enough to control them.

A great benefit to having a happy home is a father and mother who are unified in their approach to family life and who present a "unified front" to their children and the world.

2 Corinthians 13:11: Finally, brethren, farewell. Be perfect, be of good comfort, be of one mind, live in peace; and the God of love and peace shall be with you.

We firmly believe that if only one parent is willing to implement the principles in this book, they can still see great results in their family. However, we must understand that the ideal is a father and mother who are on the same page and heading the same direction. Their results will be exponentially greater.

It is critical that our children never see us disagree. We may differ on many things but we must discipline ourselves to do so privately. It will make our job of bringing our children into total subjection and obedience much easier if they know that Dad and Mom are of one mind on everything and that it is futile to attempt to play one against the other. Somehow our children instinctively know the principle of "divide and conquer" and they will use this to their advantage in skirting around the direct commands of a dad or mom. Therefore, the mother and father must have a clear plan for their children. This plan should include rules, boundaries, and expectations. Parents must act in concert to deliver and enforce these principles.

Once when one of our boys was receiving a spanking from Daddy, Mommy walked by and our little boy reached out and said, "Mommy, Mommy." She responded by taking the switch from Daddy and giving him twice the spanking he was already getting! Our children know that if they ever try to play Mommy against Daddy or vice versa, their chastisement will be double.

Fathers, we will stand before God and give an account for how well we rule our homes. Mothers, we will stand before God and give an account for how well we follow our husbands and assist and support them in ruling our homes. Children, we will stand before God and give an account for how well we obeyed and honored our parents. Let us not be found wanting.

The Courage of Convictions

♦

1 Peter 3:15
But sanctify the Lord God in your hearts: and be ready always to give an answer to every man that asketh you a reason of the hope that is in you with meekness and fear:

Each family that studies God's Word and grows spiritually as it follows Jesus will eventually begin to form certain ideals, convictions, and standards of conduct within their family. Some of these will not be popular with friends, family, and even some fellow believers. But, in light of our accountability to God for our family as discussed in the last chapter, we must stand firm and be courageous in protecting and defending these convictions.

As the vision for a godly family becomes clearer, we will of necessity begin to make decisions about such things as our children's education, standards of conduct for ourselves and our children, lifestyle choices, associations, entertainment, a church home, activities, and a host of other subjects. It is not our intention at this juncture to define or make suggestions in any of these areas but to encourage each family to prayerfully, scripturally, and with wise counsel establish convictions for your family and then stand by them no matter which direction the prevailing winds are currently blowing.

Early on in our family's growth, before homeschooling was well known or even heard of and before the current return to family-centered living that has grown out of the homeschool movement, we began to encounter much resistance from many well-meaning individuals, including family members, who could not understand why we would want to homeschool our children or have them sit with us in church instead of attending Sunday school, or many other convictions that were different from the status quo. Many of these folks were congenial about it; however, there were also those who were not so nice. Consequently, because we understood that we would stand before God for this family and frankly those people would not have to give an account for our family, we developed a strong

17

sense of what our family was about and why we believed so intensely in certain positions. We prepared ourselves to be ready always to give an answer for what God was doing in our lives and why.

It is in this area that the headship of the father really comes into play. The man can provide a shelter for his wife and children from the storm of questions, concerns, advice, and even criticisms that will arise by first taking full responsibility for his family and secondly by teaching his wife to refer all detractors directly to him. By taking responsibility, we simply mean that he takes the lead in establishing the philosophy of the family on every subject and publicly claims responsibility for said philosophy when and if it is brought into question. Thereby, he relieves his wife of having to answer for things that she has not the authority to change. God has designed that the husband to be the protector of his wife and family. He can take the pressure of the self-appointed family commentators much better than his wife can. He therefore, must teach her to simply direct those who would challenge the beliefs and actions of the family to him. It will be a great relief to her if she will learn to say, "That is a great question/suggestion. As head of our home, my husband makes those decisions/choices and establishes those precedents. Perhaps you should talk to him about it." She can do this sweetly and completely without offense, and it will stop cold those who would undermine the father's authority and alleviate the need for her to be confrontational in any way. One of the phrases that we learned years ago from a precious homeschooling family that God moved in next door to us at a critical time in the formation of our family philosophy was this: "Well, I understand your concerns, but this is what the Bullen family does." It worked so well because it wasn't accusatory or arrogant; it just simply highlighted our family autonomy and right to do with our household as we saw fit in the Lord. We even sat under pastors who thought we were hurting our children's future by not enrolling them in the local pagan seminary (public school). We always just smiled and said, "This is what we believe God wants the Bullen family to do." It wouldn't have been beneficial to contend with him because his mind was made up. When our friends and fellow believers would question our standards and we knew that they were not at a place in their growth where they would understand or accept the whole scriptural and philosophical principles behind them, we would simply say, "Well, this is just what the Bullen family feels we should do." That would be enough for most folks, and later, when they were ready, God would always open the door for us to delve further into the truth with those people. Had we blown them out of the water right off, we would never have had the opportunity to disciple them in God's plan for families later. It was also very useful when our children would question us as to why other children in our church were allowed to go to places or do certain things that our children were not allowed to do. Especially when they were very young, it was not necessary or even desirable that we explain ourselves to our kids for every action since we were training them to first submit and obey without question. When it was appropriate, we would simply say, "Remember, this is what the Bullen family does." We will discuss later in this book the importance of that identity "the Bullen family" and the "constant communication" principle that we used as they got older to teach them the convictions behind our decisions.

We should always remain teachable and we should never use our firmness of conviction as an excuse for rejecting wise counsel from godly people who have the fruit in their lives and families to validate their opinions, but we should stand firm and never waver on solid truth. The consequences of cowardice are failure and disappointment.

The danger with courage of convictions is that we are sometimes tempted to move to the other side of the spectrum and become Pharisees where our personal standards and preferences suddenly become the only right way to do things and we begin to look down on other families who don't meet our expectations. We must be careful of holding a view that whatever God is doing specifically in our family is the perfect path for all families. At that point, we will begin to judge and compare instead of love and show grace to others whom God may have other plans for. Don't get so caught up with the externals that you lose sight of the internals. Be strong, but be meek as well.

The Figure of a Father

✦

Genesis 18:19

For I know him, that he will command his children and his household after him and they shall keep the way of the LORD, to do justice and judgment; that the LORD may bring upon Abraham that which he hath spoken of him.

Fathers, can the Lord say this of us? What an awesome statement God makes concerning Father Abraham. He says some interesting things here and throughout the scripture that we can draw from in outlining "the figure of a father."

First, God says, "I know him." Now we know that God is omniscient and knows all things, but just the way he says this makes us think about the fact that God spent a lot of time with Abraham and he knew his heart. Consequently, Abraham apparently spent a lot of time with God and knew his heart as well. Fathers, be a man of God! Get to know the mind of God. Submit yourself to him in such a way that he can say, "I know him."

Second, God says, "he will command his children and his household." God knew that Abraham had embraced his calling to be the head of his family and that he would *command* his family. *Command* is some strong word, folks! As we discussed in "The Author of Authority," God put the man in charge of his family, and here we see that God could count on Abraham to command his family.

Third, God says, "after him." This is huge! Don't miss this! God not only knew Abraham and that he would command his family but also knew that Abraham was setting an example for his family. He was leading and he could command his family "after him." We must live what we preach, dads. The old saying is "More is caught than taught," and it is so true. Another one is "I'd rather see a sermon than hear one any day." Can we say with the writer in Proverbs 23:26, *"My son, give me thine heart and let thine eyes observe my ways"*? A father who says one thing and does another either will produce rebels who can't respect their

20

father and won't listen to a word he says or will raise a hypocrite who follows his example and does one thing while saying another.

Fourth, God says, "and they shall keep the way of the Lord." God makes it clear here that the result of Abraham commanding his children and household and setting an example would result in them keeping the way of the Lord. In God's universe, there is a law called "cause and effect." No matter how we try to explain it away and rationalize it, the Word makes it clear that there are consequences to actions and that the father who obeys God and leads will have certain results, and the father who abdicates and shirks his duty will have certain results. Let us fervently determine to be faithful and raise families up that will keep the way of the Lord.

Fifth, God says, "that the LORD may bring upon Abraham that which he hath spoken of him." Throughout scripture, God teaches us over and over again that if we meet the requirements for his promised blessings, he will most assuredly keep his end of the bargain and will accomplish all that he has promised to do.

In addition to what we have already gleaned from this verse, as we attempt to sketch the figure of a father, there are some obvious attributes that must be included.

I. A Good Christian

A good father will work to exhibit the fruit of the Spirit: love, joy, peace, long-suffering, gentleness, goodness, faith, meekness, and temperance. This is not some lofty, unreachable perfection we speak of but a man who by faith yields himself to the Spirit of God and strives every day to practice these graces in his life. Men, we must do battle with our flesh and trust God's Spirit to work in us these traits. Then we can bless our wives and children with a husband and father who conforms to the image of Christ. Take one of the Christian graces listed in Galatians 5:22–23: *"But the fruit of the Spirit is love, joy, peace, longsuffering, gentleness, goodness, faith, meekness, temperance: against such there is no law."* Focus on it in your life every day for a month, and at the end of nine short months you will be a different man. Your wife will feel as if she is married to Jesus and your children will feel as if they have God for a father. Romans 8:28–29 tells us that God's plan is to conform us to the image of his Son. The fruit of the Spirit shows us what that image looks like.

II. A Good Husband

Dads, you can give no greater gift to your children than to love their mother with all your heart. I am not speaking only of the romantic, Hollywood, warm, fond, affectionate love that you had when you met her but of the 1 Corinthians 13 type. Sacrificial love is an act of the will to be loving and not merely an emotion. This is the type of love that Paul is speaking of in Ephesians 5:25–31:

Husbands, love your wives, even as Christ also loved the church and gave himself for it; That he might sanctify and cleanse it with the washing of water by the word, That he might present it to himself a glorious church, not having spot, or wrinkle, or any such thing; but that it should be holy and without blemish. So ought men to love their wives as their own bodies. He that loveth his wife loveth himself. For no man ever yet hated his own flesh; but nourisheth and cherisheth it, even as the Lord the church: For we are members of his body, of his flesh and of his bones. For this cause shall a man leave his father and mother and shall be joined unto his wife and they two shall be one flesh.

Treat your wife like the gift of God that you know her to be. Love her self-lessly, washing her from every spot or wrinkle with your words. Train your sons to treat her as the angel that she is, and train your daughters to reverence her and emulate her. Love her as your own body and she will blossom into the woman of your dreams and you will bask in her glory! Your children will love and admire you for it, and you and your wife will secure a place in their hearts that nothing can destroy.

III. BE LOVING and AFFECTIONATE

A father who speaks sweet words and who hugs and kisses his wife and children regularly will have their hearts forever. Your wife needs to hear how lovely she is in your eyes. Your daughters need to hear how wonderful they are to you and what a gift from heaven they are. Your sons need to hear your approval and receive your blessing daily. Sometimes when our children get older, as dads we tend to not be as affectionate with them and this is a fatal mistake. In the Bullen family we hug and kiss and hang on each other all the time. Our girls still pile up on daddy's lap in the evening. Our boys, who are now men, still hug and kiss dad every day because daddy has never been afraid of being too affectionate to his children. Consequently he has kept their hearts.

IV. BE Humble

Dads, we are never going to be perfect but we can be humble. When we fail—and we will fail—we must be quick to humble ourselves before our wife and children and confess our wrong and ask their forgiveness. This doesn't sound like a very manly thing to do, but be assured that it is a key to our wife's and our child's heart; when we rise up from that place of humility and contrition, we will stand ten feet taller in their eyes. We may have many flaws and areas for growth, but our family will follow us to the death if we do not try to cover for, rationalize, and excuse our faults instead of just sincerely confessing and forsaking them.

V. KEEP YOUR WORD

A good dad must keep his promises. Our wives and children must know in their hearts that we are men of our word. A father who is not trustworthy will lose the respect of his children. If he makes a vow and doesn't keep it, even in the smallest things, they will eventually cease to listen to him in the important things as well. Therefore, we must be careful what we promise and only break one if it is under dire circumstances; even then we must ask their forgiveness so that when something very important comes along and we really need them to listen to us and believe us, we won't find that they have tuned us out long ago because our word was of no value.

VI. BE STEEL and VELVET

A good dad must be both soft and tender and at the same time strong and firm. He must be rock solid in disciplining and correcting his children. He must be unmovable and steadfast in enforcing the standards of conduct set down for his children. But, at the same time, he must be gentle and compassionate when teaching and training. He must be patient and long-suffering as he nurtures and brings up his children in the admonition of the Lord. He must be fearsome and dreadful to the enemies of his family's unity in his role as protector but at the same time kind and sweet in his affections to his children and their mother. He is, for good or bad, a picture of God the Father in the home, and his presence should inspire reverence and respect as well as love and devotion.

VII. BE A Servant

Lead by example. A good dad will work harder, love more, give more, serve more, and try harder than he ever requires from his wife and children, and consequently they will be drawn to him as dear followers rather than driven before him as a herd of beasts.

VIII. LAST BUT Certainly NOT LEAST, BE HOLY

Be vigilant to keep your mind and body from succumbing to the lusts of the flesh. Be transparent with your family and your friends. Abhor pretense and facades of every kind. Live so that your daughters would not be ashamed if they could read your mind. Live so that you would be overjoyed if your daughters married someone just like you. Live so that you would be proud if your sons grew up to be just like you. Look into the eyes of your little ones and determine in your heart that you would die before you would betray them or their mother for some momentary, fleshly pleasure. Pour the Word into your mind constantly. Reach out by faith and accept Christ's victory over sin that he wrought for you at the cross and through his resurrection. Salvation is by faith alone and sanctification is by faith alone as well. The Lord didn't just save us from sin and then leave us here to wrestle with it on our own. He overcame sin completely at the cross, and when we are baptized into Christ by the Holy Spirit, we become partakers in that triumph. Believe God when he says you are dead to sin and reach out to him in faith, and he will give you victory and freedom like you have never known.

Romans 6:1–7: What shall we say then? Shall we continue in sin, that grace may abound? God forbid. How shall we, that __are__ dead to sin, live any longer therein? Know ye not, that so many of us as were baptized into Jesus Christ were baptized into his death? Therefore we __are__ buried with him by baptism into death: that like as Christ was raised up from the dead by the glory of the Father, even so we also should walk in newness of life. For if we have been planted together in the likeness of his death, we shall be also in the likeness of his resurrection: Knowing this, that our old man __is__ crucified with him, that the body of sin might be destroyed, that henceforth we should not serve sin. For he that __is__ dead __is__ freed from sin.

Just like with salvation, in sanctification Jesus has already done all of the work; our response is simple faith, which then brings the victory.

The Wisdom of a Wife

✦

Proverbs 19:14
House and riches are the inheritance of fathers: and a prudent wife is from the LORD.

Proverbs 31:10–12, 26
Who can find a virtuous woman? for her price is far above rubies. The heart of her husband doth safely trust in her, so that he shall have no need of spoil. She will do him good and not evil all the days of her life. She openeth her mouth with wisdom; and in her tongue is the law of kindness.

Proverbs 14:1
Every wise woman buildeth her house: but the foolish plucketh it down with her hands.

What would the blessed family be without the wife and mother of the home? We shudder to think. God, in his incredible wisdom, created man and then created a helper for him, which Adam named "woman." The Bible has much to say about the impact that a woman has on her home for either good or evil. Perhaps the greatest asset to any happy home is a woman of wisdom. God has created within a woman an amazing power to influence those around her. She ultimately sets the mood and establishes the "atmosphere" of the home. She can build up with her words or tear down with a single look. She can make her man into a hero of dynamic proportions, or she can whittle him down to a mere shadow of his former self. She can motivate and inspire her children to greatness, or she can discourage and belittle them to frustration. She can create a home where peace and harmony are the order of the day, or she can create a home where, as the writer of Proverbs states, *"It is better to dwell in a corner of the housetop, than with a brawling woman in a wide house"* (Proverbs 21:9). She can open her mouth with wisdom, or she can be as the Word again says, *"And the contentions of a wife are a continual dropping"* (Proverbs 19:13), or *"It is better to dwell in the wilderness, than with a contentious and an angry woman"* (Proverbs 21:19), or *"A continual drop-ping in a very rainy day and a contentious woman are alike"* (Proverbs 27:15). But a virtuous woman is a very valuable treasure! Ladies, we can with our words, with our looks, and with our attitudes create for ourselves and for our families a haven of joy and rest or a nest of discontentment, complaint, and disappointment. It is our choice.

The wisdom of a wife begins with the heart. A wife and mother must first and foremost commit her heart and the issues of it to Christ. She must, by faith, yield the thoughts and intents of her heart to God and bring them into obedience to his Word. She must guard her heart always against the fruit of the flesh and work to exhibit the fruit of the Spirit. She must fill her heart and mind with the Word of God so that it is renewed and washed and filled with the wisdom of God so that she can be the wife and mother God designed her to be.

The wisdom of a wife becomes most evident in her speech.

Luke 6:45: *A good man out of the good treasure of his heart bringeth forth that which is good; and an evil man out of the evil treasure of his heart bringeth forth that which is evil: for of the abundance of the heart his mouth speaketh.*

James said the tongue is an unruly evil. Proverbs 31:26 really nails it when it says of the virtuous woman, *"She openeth her mouth with wisdom; and in her tongue is the law of kindness."* Ladies, we build up our husbands, children, and homes with our tongue. Learn to bite your tongue when you are tempted to speak those things that don't reflect the wisdom of God.

Philippians 4:8: *Finally, brethren, whatsoever things are true, whatsoever things are honest, whatsoever things are just, whatsoever things are pure, whatsoever things are lovely, whatsoever things are of good report; if there be any virtue and if there be any praise, think on these things.*

Ladies, flee from the three C's: Criticize, Condemn, Complain. No good can come from these three, but much damage can result.

Add these three: Praise, Approve, Thank. There will of course be many times when we must be firm and be willing to stand our ground and wield the rod of correction with strength and honor, but we never have to stoop to the three C's.

Moms, be cheerful! You can fail at many things in the home and not ruin your children, but if you fail at being cheerful, nothing else will matter. Children can overcome living in a messy house, a less-than-average education, or a less-than-perfect diet, but there is no overcoming the lack of a cheerful mom. The Bible uses the earthly family as a picture or representation of the Godhead (Father, Son, Holy Spirit). Well, ladies, in that analogy, the Holy Spirit would be repre-sented by the wife and mother of the family. Let's look for a moment at the attributes and work of the Holy Spirit and see how they relate to the attributes and work of a godly wife and mother.

First, the Holy Spirit is called the comforter.

John 14:26: *But the Comforter, which is the Holy Ghost, whom the Father will send in my name, he shall teach you all things and bring all things to your remembrance, whatsoever I have said unto you.*

John 16:7: *Nevertheless I tell you the truth; It is expedient for you that I go away: for if I go not away, the Comforter will not come unto you; but if I depart, I will send him unto you.*

John 14:16: *And I will pray the Father and he shall give you another Comforter, that he may abide with you for ever;*

Likewise, a wife and mother is the comforter and nurturer of the home.

Second, the Holy Spirit is a teacher.

John 14:26: *But the Comforter, which is the Holy Ghost, whom the Father will send in my name, he shall teach you all things and bring all things to your remembrance, whatsoever I have said unto you.*

John 15:26: *But when the Comforter is come, whom I will send unto you from the Father, even the Spirit of truth, which proceedeth from the Father, he shall testify of me.*

Likewise, a wife and mother is to teach, train, and testify of Jesus to her family.

Third, the Holy Spirit is always behind the scenes, reflecting the glory back to God.

John 16:13: *Howbeit when he, the Spirit of truth, is come, he will guide you into all truth: for he shall not speak of himself; but whatsoever he shall hear, that shall he speak: and he will shew you things to come. He shall glorify me: for he shall receive of mine and shall shew it unto you.*

Likewise, a wife and mother spends most of her time in the background doing her work quietly. She is not on the stage or in the pulpit. She is at home teaching, training, and speaking those things that edify the children and build up her husband. She doesn't speak of herself or gather to herself much glory. However, she is the power behind all good that comes out of her home.

Fourth, the Holy Spirit intercedes.

Romans 8:27: *And he that searcheth the hearts knoweth what is the mind of the Spirit, because he maketh intercession for the saints according to the will of God.*

Likewise, a wife and mother intercedes before God for her husband and her children.

Ladies, you are the holy spirit of your home. You set the atmosphere. You lead, guide, convict, reveal, admonish, and encourage just like the Holy Spirit of God! Never allow the deceiver to make you feel insignificant and helpless to change the world. Your husband may be the head, but you are the neck. You determine whether he succeeds or fails. You can make him or break him. An old preacher once told us, "Men may build churches, but the women determine whether they are happy while they do it." You wield an incredible power in the universe. The old adage "The hand that rocks the cradle, rules the world" is so true. Your home needs a queen, ladies. Paul the Apostle said, *"I will therefore that the younger women marry, bear children, guide the house, give none occasion to the adversary to speak reproachfully"* (1 Timothy 5:14). The Greek word used here for "guides the house" is *oikodespoteo*. It literally means to rule the home or be master of the house. You are a queen! You rule a kingdom!

Proverbs 31:27: *She looketh well to the ways of her household and eateth not the bread of idleness.*

You may not know this, but your bathrobe is a royal robe and your spatula is a scepter. You are not a second-class citizen because you have chosen to follow God and be a housewife and mother. Your husband is out slaying the dragons and taking dominion for Christ and he needs a queen to rule the castle. Look at the woman in Proverbs 31. She was no doormat.

Proverbs 31:25: *Strength and honour are her clothing; and she shall rejoice in time to come.*

She is a ruler in a kingdom and she does it so well that her husband's place among the elders at the gate of the city is enhanced by her virtue and influence.

Proverbs 31:23: *Her husband is known in the gates, when he sitteth among the elders of the land.*

Young mother, you may be working away in obscurity right now, but if you are faithful to your calling as queen of that home, your day is coming and you will rejoice in time to come. The blessedness is coming for you.

Proverbs 31:28–31: *Her children arise up and call her blessed; her husband also and he praiseth her. Many daughters have done virtuously, but thou excellest them all. Favour is deceitful and beauty is vain: but a woman that feareth the LORD, she shall be praised. Give her of the fruit of her hands; and let her own works praise her in the gates.*

The Health of the Heart

$\blacklozenge$

1 Samuel 16:7
But the LORD said unto Samuel, Look not on his countenance, or on the height of his stature; because I have refused him: for the LORD seeth not as man seeth; for man looketh on the outward appearance, but the LORD looketh on the heart.

In building a generation that brings glory to God, we must focus on the heart. The importance of this topic cannot be overstated. All of the other subjects that we have and will cover are inherently bound to this one because out of our hearts flow all the issues of life. Every parent who loses their child to the world first lost their heart somewhere along the way.

Matthew 12:34–35: O generation of vipers, how can ye, being evil, speak good things? for out of the abundance of the heart the mouth speaketh. A good man out of the good treasure of the heart bringeth forth good things: and an evil man out of the evil treasure of the heart bringeth forth evil things.

Matthew 15:18–19: But those things which proceed out of the mouth come forth from the heart; and they defile the man. For out of the heart proceed evil thoughts, murders, adulteries, fornications, thefts, false witness, blasphemies:

1 Timothy 1:5: Now the end of the commandment is charity out of a pure heart and of a good conscience and of faith unfeigned:

2 Timothy 2:22: Flee also youthful lusts: but follow righteousness, faith, charity, peace, with them that call on the Lord out of a pure heart.

As the Lord told Samuel, he looks on the heart. It is his main concern, and yet we find ourselves many times worrying about and working on the outside to the neglect of the inside altogether. We can look like a "godly family." We can dress like a "godly family." We can go where "godly families" go. We can use the catch-phrases that "godly families" use. We can homeschool and adopt a "family-friendly lifestyle." We can even genuinely desire to have a family that glorifies God, but if our hearts and the hearts of our children are full of pride, envy, malice, anger, bitterness, gossip, self-will, ingratitude, fear, lust, strife, self-indul-gence, slothfulness, and so on, these fruits will ultimately manifest themselves outwardly, our children will rebel, our marriages will fail, and the world will say, "Wow, they did everything right and still lost their children." "I guess Proverbs 22:6 [*"Train up a child in the way he should go: and when he is old, he will not depart from it"*] must mean something else other than what it clearly says." Worse yet, we may raise a family of Pharisees who have all of the superficial characteris-tics of Christianity but are self-absorbed and proud and their only contribution to the kingdom of Christ is to be the self-appointed judge of God's people. On the other hand, if our hearts and the hearts of our children are full of love, joy, peace, faith, gentleness, goodness, meekness, mercy, humility, diligence, and self-lessness, the outward self will be easy to conform to the ways of the Lord.

One of the greatest experiences that God ever gave the Bullen family was a Bible study we did together on the fruit of the Spirit listed in Galatians 5:22–23. We took each word and studied the root meanings in the original languages. We looked at all of the synonyms of each word and every place in the New Testament where it was used. For a couple of weeks we looked at, talked about, prayed about, and focused on these Christian graces and each of us searched our own hearts. We began to be more sensitive to how we were exhibiting the fruit of the flesh listed in Galatians 5:19–21, and we set out, by faith, to work on displaying the good fruit. This study dramatically changed all of our lives and our family. We have gone back and reviewed what we learned many, many times so that we keep our hearts and minds fresh with God's dynamic truth.

Because we realize that all behavior emanates from the heart, when we as par-ents begin to see actions or attitudes in our children that don't line up with God's will and ways, instead of just attacking and addressing the specific conduct, we always start with the heart and find out where our child left the path. It would be easier to just exercise our parental authority and make them straighten up, but we have come to realize that their demeanor is simply a warning sign that all is not well with the heart. If we do not help them to cleanse their mind, heart, and con-science and restore their heart to a right relationship with us and the Lord, some-day they will be too old to care about our authority and we will have lost them.

Dr. S.M. Davis in his sermon "Winning the Heart of a Rebel" says that the most important thing you will ever hear a preacher say in reference to child rear-ing is, "Win the heart of your child early, keep that child's heart diligently, and if you ever discover that you have lost their heart, retrace your steps and find where you lost it and heal the breech. Whoever has your child's heart controls their life."

If a teenager wants to look like and dress like their friends rather than the way mom and dad desire, if a teenager wants to spend time with their friends rather than spending time with the family, if they talk to and listen to their friends rather than talk to and listen to mom and dad, then their peers have their heart and not mom and dad.

Proverbs 23:26: *My son, give me thine heart, and let thine eyes observe my ways.*

A father and mother who have won the heart of their daughter and who carefully keep that heart never have to worry about some less than desirable young man coming along and leading their daughter astray. She is secure in her mommy and daddy's love and approval and therefore is not vulnerable and susceptible to being corrupted. A father and mother who have won the heart of their son and who diligently keep that heart never have to worry about their son being drawn away by less than desirable companions because whoever has his heart is who influences him.

In the same message, Dr. Davis points out that Absalom won the hearts of the men of Israel away his father, King David, by three things: (1) he listened to them, (2) he talked to them, and (3) he touched them.

2 Samuel 15:2–6: *And Absalom rose up early, and stood beside the way of the gate: and it was so, that when any man that had a controversy came to the king for judgment, then Absalom called unto him, and said, Of what city art thou? And he said, Thy servant is of one of the tribes of Israel. And Absalom said unto him, See, thy matters are good and right; but there is no man deputed of the king to hear thee. Absalom said moreover, Oh that I were made judge in the land, that every man which hath any suit or cause might come unto me, and I would do him justice! And it was [so], that when any man came nigh [to him] to do him obeisance, he put forth his hand, and took him, and kissed him. And on this manner did Absalom to all Israel that came to the king for judgment: so Absalom stole the hearts of the men of Israel.*

The way to win and keep our children's hearts is through fellowship. It is through spending time with, loving, accepting, praising, approving of, and being interested in our children that we secure their hearts.

The two best ways to lose our child's heart are anger and neglect.

Ephesians 6:4 *And, ye fathers, provoke not your children to wrath: but bring them up in the nurture and admonition of the Lord.*

Colossians 3:21 *Fathers, provoke not your children to anger, lest they be discouraged.*

We will deal with more of the practical issues of how we affect our and our children's hearts for the Lord in the next several chapters, but let us realize that this must be the focus of all of our training, teaching, and correction, or it will all be for naught. We must never be satisfied that outwardly we appear to be a "good

Christian family." Our goal must be to *"follow righteousness, faith, charity, peace, with them that call on the Lord out of a pure heart" (2 Tim. 2:22).*

The Law of Love

✦

James 2:8
If ye fulfil the royal law according to the scripture, Thou shalt love thy neighbour as thyself, ye do well:

As we enter into this discussion of love, we feel like Moses at the burning bush when God told him to remove his shoes for he was standing on holy ground.

Love is the theme of the Christian life. It is the very heart of God. It is the hallmark of a blessed family. It is the greatest power for change in this world.

James called it the "royal law." Jesus said that by love the world will know that we are his.

John 13:35: *By this shall all men know that ye are my disciples, if ye have love one to another.*

Jesus said that love was the first and second greatest commandments and the epitome of all that was contained in the entire Old Testament.

Matthew 22:37–40: *Jesus said unto him, Thou shalt love the Lord thy God with all thy heart and with all thy soul and with all thy mind. This is the first and great commandment. And the second is like unto it, Thou shalt love thy neighbour as thyself. On these two commandments hang all the law and the prophets.*

At the conclusion of his Sermon on the Mount in Matthew 5–7, Jesus sums it all up in Matthew 7:12: *"Therefore all things whatsoever ye would that men should do to you, do ye even so to them: for this is the law and the prophets."* When we read the Sermon on the Mount in the context of Jesus telling us that loving our neighbor is the fulfillment of the law, we can see why those Jews who were present there that day and heard that sermon said, *"And it came to pass, when Jesus had ended these sayings, the people were astonished at his doctrine: For he taught them as one having authority and not as the scribes"* (Matt. 7:28–29). Here was a man who was teaching that if you loved your neighbor as yourself, you had kept all the law

33

and the prophets! To a Jew, this was astonishing doctrine. Look at this discourse between Jesus and a scribe in Mark 12:28–34:

And one of the scribes came and having heard them reasoning together and perceiving that he had answered them well, asked him, Which is the first commandment of all? And Jesus answered him, The first of all the commandments is, Hear, O Israel; The Lord our God is one Lord: And thou shalt love the Lord thy God with all thy heart and with all thy soul and with all thy mind and with all thy strength: this is the first commandment. And the second is like, namely this, Thou shalt love thy neighbour as thyself. There is none other commandment greater than these. And the scribe said unto him, Well, Master, thou hast said the truth: for there is one God; and there is none other but he: And to love him with all the heart and with all the understanding and with all the soul and with all the strength and to love his neighbour as himself, is more than all whole burnt offerings and sacrifices. And when Jesus saw that he answered discreetly, he said unto him, Thou art not far from the kingdom of God. And no man after that durst ask him any question.

Paul also expounds on this in Romans 13:8–10:

Owe no man any thing, but to love one another: for he that loveth another hath fulfilled the law. For this, Thou shalt not commit adultery, Thou shalt not kill, Thou shalt not steal, Thou shalt not bear false witness, Thou shalt not covet; and if there be any other commandment, it is briefly comprehended in this saying, namely, Thou shalt love thy neighbour as thyself. Love worketh no ill to his neighbour: therefore love is the fulfilling of the law.

And again Paul says in Galatians 5:14: *"For all the law is fulfilled in one word, even in this; Thou shalt love thy neighbour as thyself."* Or, in Galatians 6:2: *"Bear ye one another's burdens and so fulfil the law of Christ."*

Paul said that love was the greatest of the Christian graces.

1 Corinthians 13:13: *And now abideth faith, hope, charity, these three; but the greatest of these is charity.*

John said that it was the true mark of a child of God.

1 John 4:7–8: *Beloved, let us love one another: for love is of God; and every one that loveth is born of God and knoweth God. He that loveth not knoweth not God; for God is love.*

Peter put love above all things.

1 Peter 4:8: *And above all things have fervent charity among yourselves: for charity shall cover the multitude of sins.*

Paul also put love above all things in Colossians 3:14: *"And above all these things put on charity, which is the bond of perfectness."* It's hard to imagine a more succinct commentary on the importance of love than Paul's in 1 Corinthians 13:1–8:

Though I speak with the tongues of men and of angels and have not charity, I am become as sounding brass, or a tinkling cymbal. And though I have the gift of prophecy and understand all mysteries and all knowledge; and though I have all faith, so that I could remove mountains and have not charity, I am nothing. And though I bestow all my goods to feed the poor and though I give my body to be burned and have not charity, it profiteth me nothing. Charity suffereth long, and is kind; charity envieth not; charity vaunteth not itself, is not puffed up, doth not behave itself unseemly, seeketh not her own, is not easily provoked, thinketh no evil; Rejoiceth not in iniquity, but rejoiceth in the truth; Beareth all things, believeth all things, hopeth all things, endureth all things. Charity never faileth: but whether there be prophecies, they shall fail; whether there be tongues, they shall cease; whether there be knowledge, it shall vanish away

With such superlative statements in God's word, it is not hard to figure out what is of supreme importance to God and consequently what should be of supreme importance to us and our families. We once explained it in this way when counseling someone who was struggling with Pharisaism: "If you were starting out as a new believer and you wanted to know what was required of you and so you went to the Bible and found out what it talked about the most and worked on that first until you had it down and then moved down the list until you finally reached the obscure and even controversial passages of scripture, before you got past the first thing on the list, which is love God and love others, you would find that all of the other things on the list had been met in you as you fulfilled the first one. The cultist does the opposite. He starts with the obscure and controversial and builds a whole belief system upon it." Name any sin and you will discover that the root of that sin is either not loving God or not loving others. This is why God says over and over again in the verses listed above and dozens of others that love is the most important thing! If we miss this, all of our works are wood, hay, and stubble. This is why Jesus could say that all of the law and the prophets hang on loving God and loving others. Likewise, all of Christ's commandments in the New Testament can be summarized by "love God and love one another as well."

Galatians 6:2: *Bear ye one another's burdens and so fulfil the law of Christ.*

John 13:34: *A new commandment I give unto you, That ye love one another; as I have loved you, that ye also love one another.*

John 15:12: *This is my commandment, That ye love one another, as I have loved you.*

Romans 13:9b: and if there be any other commandment, it is briefly comprehended in this saying, namely, Thou shalt love thy neighbour as thyself.

1John 3:23: And this is his commandment, That we should believe on the name of his Son Jesus Christ and love one another, as he gave us commandment.

1John 4:21: And this commandment have we from him, That he who loveth God love his brother also.

2 John 1:5–6: And now I beseech thee, lady, not as though I wrote a new commandment unto thee, but that which we had from the beginning, that we love one another. And this is love, that we walk after his commandments. This is the commandment, That, as ye have heard from the beginning, ye should walk in it.

Romans 12:10: Be kindly affectioned one to another with brotherly love; in honour preferring one another;

Ephesians 5:1–2: Be ye therefore followers of God, as dear children; And walk in love, as Christ also hath loved us and hath given himself for us an offering and a sacrifice to God for a sweetsmelling savour.

1 Thessalonians 3:12–13 And the Lord make you to increase and abound in love one toward another and toward all men, even as we do toward you: To the end he may stablish your hearts unblameable in holiness before God, even our Father, at the coming of our Lord Jesus Christ with all his saints.

1 Thessalonians 4:9–10 But as touching brotherly love ye need not that I write unto you: for ye yourselves are taught of God to love one another. And indeed ye do it toward all the brethren which are in all Macedonia: but we beseech you, brethren, that ye increase more and more;

1 Timothy 1:5: Now the end of the commandment is charity out of a pure heart and of a good conscience and of faith unfeigned:

1Peter 1:22: Seeing ye have purified your souls in obeying the truth through the Spirit unto unfeigned love of the brethren, see that ye love one another with a pure heart fervently:

1Peter 3:8: Finally, be ye all of one mind, having compassion one of another, love as brethren, be pitiful, be courteous:

1 John 4:11–13: Beloved, if God so loved us, we ought also to love one another. No man hath seen God at any time. If we love one another, God dwelleth in us and his love is perfected in us. Hereby know we that we dwell in him and he in us, because he hath given us of his Spirit.

1 John 3:10–18: In this the children of God are manifest, and the children of the devil: whosoever doeth not righteousness is not of God, neither he that loveth not his brother. For this is the message that ye heard from the beginning, that we should love one another. Not as Cain, who was of that wicked one, and slew his brother. And wherefore slew he him? Because his own works were evil, and his brother's righteous. Marvel not, my brethren, if the world hate you. We know that we have passed from death unto life, because we love the brethren. He that loveth not his brother abideth in death. Whosoever hateth his brother is a murderer: and ye know that no murderer hath eternal life abiding in him. Hereby perceive we the love of God, because he laid down his life for us: and we ought to lay down our lives for the brethren. But whoso hath this world's good, and seeth his brother have need, and shutteth up his bowels of compassion from him, how dwelleth the love of God in him? My little children, let us not love in word, neither in tongue; but in deed and in truth.

1 John 2:3–11: *And hereby we do know that we know him, if we keep his commandments. He that saith, I know him, and keepeth not his commandments, is a liar, and the truth is not in him. But whoso keepeth his word, in him verily is the love of God perfected: hereby know we that we are in him. He that saith he abideth in him ought himself also so to walk, even as he walked. Brethren, I write no new commandment unto you, but an old commandment which ye had from the beginning. The old commandment is the word which ye have heard from the beginning. Again, a new commandment I write unto you, which thing is true in him and in you: because the darkness is past, and the true light now shineth. He that saith he is in the light, and hateth his brother, is in darkness even until now. He that loveth his brother abideth in the light, and there is none occasion of stumbling in him. But he that hateth his brother is in darkness, and walketh in darkness, and knoweth not whither he goeth, because that darkness hath blinded his eyes.*

"We may be certain that whatever God has made prominent in his word, he intended to be conspicuous in our lives."
—Charles Spurgeon

Here is an interesting story told by Rev. J. C. Robertson, M.A., Canon of Canterbury, in his book, *Sketches of Church History:*

> St. John lived to about the age of a hundred. He was at last so weak that he could not walk into the church; so he was carried in, and used to say continually to his people, "Little children, love one another." Some of them, after a time, began to be tired of hearing this, and asked him why he repeated the words so often, and said nothing else to them. The Apostle answered, "Because it is the Lord's commandment, and if this be done it is enough."

This is our high calling in Christ that we love God and love others. This is the true work of God! This must be the focus, the mission and the passion of our family. This love is not something that happens to us, this is not infatuation, this is giving, serving love. This is the love that is an act of our will, by faith. This is why God can command us to love and can hold us accountable for not doing so. We cannot always control our emotions, but this is not an emotion. This is a decision to act in a certain way. When Jesus says *"Greater love hath no man than this, that a man lay down his life for his friends."* (John 15:13) He is showing us that the more love we have the more selfless we will be. He defined ultimate love as an action "laying down his life." When we love God with all our heart, mind, soul and strength it manifests itself in our decisions to follow him and delight in him and live for him and speak of him and spend time with him. When we love others, it is manifest in our actions, how we treat them, how we serve them.

This is why God can command us to love our enemies. he is not saying, "have warm feelings of affection for them," he is saying "be loving" to them. The wonderful thing is that when we obey God and decide to be loving, he makes the emotions follow and we will truly feel love for God and for others. But if we wait for the feeling before we act we will never obey. When we step out on faith to follow God's word and admit to him our weakness and inability to do what he asks in our own strength, he comes and loves through us and we become a conduit for God's love to flow through to the world.

Loving God and loving others is a commandment, not a suggestion; therefore, it is a sin to do otherwise. We think of "sin" so many times as those heinous deeds of the flesh such as adultery, fornication, drunkenness, murder, theft, and so on, and rightly so, but how much greater a sin to break the great commandment. We don't think of the sin of being unloving as a dark, deep, ugly sin, but we focus on the outside. God is more concerned with the heart. All sin is a result of not loving God and our neighbor as we should, and so it is a very serious sin. It involves breaking the two greatest commandments. Do we think of this when we are sharp with each other, when we are impatient or unkind, or when we speak an unkind word about a brother or sister in Christ? We should see it and feel it as such and we must repent.

Our closest "neighbors" that we are to love are those of our own households. Husbands are specifically commanded to love their wives in Ephesians 5:25–33: *Husbands, love your wives, even as Christ also loved the church, and gave himself for it; That he might sanctify and cleanse it with the washing of water by the word, That he might present it to himself a glorious church, not having spot, or wrinkle, or any such thing; but that it should be holy and without blemish. So ought men to love their wives as their own bodies. He that loveth his wife loveth himself. For no man ever yet hated his own flesh; but nourisheth and cherisheth it, even as the Lord the church: For we are members of his body, of his flesh, and of his bones. For this cause shall a man leave his father and mother, and shall be joined unto his wife, and they two shall be one flesh. This is a great mystery: but I speak concerning Christ and the church. Nevertheless let every one of you in particular so love his wife even as himself; and the wife see that she reverence her husband.*

Paul told Titus when referring to the role of older women in the church, *"That they may teach the young women to be sober, to love their husbands, to love their children"* (Titus 2:4). This was a love that could be taught, not just the natural feelings of a wife and mother. Brothers and sisters must be taught to love one another. Again this is speaking of actions; we must teach and train them to "be loving" to one another in word and deed. Children must be taught to love their parents and likewise parents their children. Our families, homes, and ministries need to be a wellspring of love through which God can touch the world. Our children may tire of our speeches. They may outgrow their fear of us. They may grow weary of our "dead religions." But they cannot resist unrelenting godly love. Show them a religion that is based on the selfless love of Jesus as poured out through the fruit of the Spirit, which is love, joy, peace, gentleness, goodness, faith, meekness, and temperance, and they will give themselves by faith to live and die for this kind of religion.

In the early days of the Bullen family, our parenting mostly involved discipline. We were so determined to have "good" children that we were way out of balance. We did have very obedient and disciplined kids, but there was not near enough praise, cheerfulness, and old-fashioned affection. Then one day we heard an old preacher on a cassette tape say, "You can be as hard on your children as you want, you can require of them a standard of discipline that is very strict indeed, and they will never rebel as long as you heap love and affection upon them to the same degree that you discipline them." Our eyes were opened and this has been a bedrock truth for our family ever since. As father and mother of the Bullen family, we have great expectations for our children and we hold them to a very high standard of behavior, and yet they are very happy, contented, joyful, and grateful and they love and respect us immensely because we heap upon them love and affection to the same degree. Matthew's mother says it quaintly: "My secret to raising good children is love on one end of them and beat on the other end." Most parents err on one side or the other. They "love" too much and do not govern their children firmly enough, so these unfortunate children grow up self-indulged and self-absorbed and with little character; or the parents are very strict and demanding without enough love and affection, and these unfortunate children grow up to be bitter and resentful and eventually rebel. Michael

Pearl says that effective child training stands on two legs: fellowship and discipline. Through love we secure and keep their hearts, and through discipline we shape and forge their character.

The family who is consumed with loving God, loving each other, and loving others will enjoy an incredibly pleasurable existence and will be truly blessed. They will also be loved by everyone who knows them, for, as the saying goes, "The size of the window you receive through is the size of the window you give through."

The next set of "neighbors" that we should love is our brothers and sisters in the body of Christ. In our church in Magnolia, Texas, where we serve, we focus a great deal on loving and serving each other. We call it "covenantal community." As did the first church in Acts 2, we strive to live life together and have all things common in one accord. In other words, when one of us is moving, we are all there to move. When one of us is having a baby, we are all having a baby. When one of us is sick, we are all sick together and comfort and pray for the one who is ill. If a tree falls in our yard, it is *our* problem, and the men of the church flock to help remove the tree. We live life together: the good and the bad. If one of our young people is having a hard time, we all love on and pray for and encourage that young person and their parents. We bring meals to them, find jobs for them, pay unexpected bills for them, and generally strive to love our brothers and sisters as ourselves.

There are also those "neighbors" outside of our church who reside in our community and city. When the man down the street complains about our dog, he is not prepared for us to respond in love and humility. It can be a wonderful witness to him if we will love him as Jesus would.

Of course, we could name many more areas where the powerful and marvelous tool of love can be used, but the last "neighbor" we will mention are our enemies. Jesus said that we are to love even those who misuse and malign us. We believe that loving our enemies is one of the greatest ways to love Jesus because we are ultimately loving him through them.

Matthew 5:38–48: Ye have heard that it hath been said, An eye for an eye, and a tooth for a tooth: But I say unto you, That ye resist not evil: but whosoever shall smite thee on thy right cheek, turn to him the other also. And if any man will sue thee at the law, and take away thy coat, let him have thy cloke also. And whosoever shall compel thee to go a mile, go with him twain. Give to him that asketh thee, and from him that would borrow of thee turn not thou away. Ye have heard that it hath been said, Thou shalt love thy neighbour, and hate thine enemy. But I say unto you, Love your enemies, bless them that curse you, do good to them that hate you, and pray for them which despitefully use you, and persecute you; That ye may be the children of your Father which is in heaven: for he maketh his sun to rise on the evil and on the good, and sendeth rain on the just and on the unjust. For if ye love them which love you, what reward have ye? do not even the publicans the same? And if ye salute your breth-ren only, what do ye more than others? do not even the publicans so? Be ye therefore perfect, even as your Father which is in heaven is perfect.

Imagine a world where people believed and lived this. Imagine a city where all the people embraced and practiced this. Imagine a church where everyone loved each other as they loved themselves. Imagine a family where this was the norm. Wouldn't it be blessed? This, by the way, is why Christianity conquered the great Roman Empire without a single battle: love.

The Washing of the Word

✦

Psalm 119:9–11
BETH. Wherewithal shall a young man cleanse his way? by taking heed thereto according to thy word. With my whole heart have I sought thee: O let me not wander from thy commandments. Thy word have I hid in mine heart, that I might not sin against thee.

Our greatest tool in shaping our family into the vision that we spoke of in Chapter 1 is the Bible. As we pour the Word of God into ourselves and our children, the Spirit of God uses it to mold, shape, and conform us into the image of Jesus. So many times we try all of man's ideas and methods instead of just pouring the Word into our children and letting the sword of the Spirit do its work.

From birth, we should read the Word to our babies (the Holy Spirit will translate; he knows baby talk). As they grow older, maybe three or four years old, begin to memorize scripture together. Be patient and use much repetition. Memorize scriptures that relate to their everyday experiences and the things that you are currently teaching and training them about. For instance, loving their brother or sister is a wonderful subject. We made Ephesians 4:32—*"And be ye kind one to another, tenderhearted, forgiving one another, even as God for Christ's sake hath forgiven you"*—our family verse, and we all quote it to each other hundreds of times a year. By the time your children start school, they will know dozens of verses by heart, and by the time they hit their teen years, they will know hundreds of verses by heart.

The Bible is the answer for every challenge. When we would begin to see a certain character flaw showing in our children, we would collect all of the verses in scripture on that subject and memorize them together. When we identified certain virtues that we wanted to train into our children, we would again find all of the texts that related to that virtue and we memorized them together. One of the greatest blessings ever to come upon our family was putting to memory 1 Corin-

42

thians 13, the love chapter. It literally transformed our family! Throughout the epistles, Paul repeatedly lists the fruit of the Spirit, the most famous list being in Galatians 5:22–23. A few years ago, as we memorized all of these lists, a small revival broke out in our family! We began to confess our sins of being unloving to each other, and the Lord knitted our souls together like never before. The verses that we start each of these chapters with are portions that we have put to memory over the years, and they have helped us form many of the truths that we are sharing in this book. We have memorized all of the verses in Proverbs on child training and correction. We are memorizing all of the scriptures in Proverbs on sexual purity, and there are more than you would think.

What are the doctrines that are precious to us and that we want our children to be strong in? What are the values and virtues that are precious to us and we want to see in our children?

What behavioral challenges are we having with our kids or with ourselves for that matter? Memorize and meditate on the scriptures pertaining to these subjects and see what the Word, which is alive and powerful and sharper than any sword, can do! Have little boys memorize verses in the Bible that pertain to manhood, and likewise have little girls memorize those that pertain to womanhood.

There seems to be a phenomenon in our brains that the more we memorize the easier it is to memorize, and so eventually we memorized entire chapters. Now we are working on memorizing whole books of the Bible. Don't be overwhelmed; start small, just a verse a week, or a month, but get the Word into their hearts and minds.

Our favorite definition of wisdom is *seeing things as God sees them*. In order for us to see things as God sees them, we must know how God sees them, and the place to learn that is the Bible. As we fill our minds and hearts with his Word, we will begin to think like him and see things as he sees them. We will grow in wisdom, knowledge, and understanding and become more useful to the kingdom of God. Pour the Word of God into your hearts and minds continually.

The Triumph or the Tragedy

✦

Proverbs 10:1

The proverbs of Solomon. A wise son maketh a glad father: but a foolish son is the heaviness of his mother.

Why do some children who grow up in a "Christian home" turn out good (wise) and others choose the world over the faith of their parents and turn out bad (fools)? This is a question that we often hear. The answer is clearly found in the book of Proverbs. Proverbs is a divinely inspired collection of writings from a father to his son. This father (King Solomon) laid down all that he desired for his son to know about life in this book. He drew stark comparisons between the fool and the wise man and gave his son brilliant yet practical advice on how to be one and avoid being the other. He also taught his son how to raise his own children to be wise and not fools. Solomon says in Proverbs 22:6, *"Train up a child in the way he should go: and when he is old, he will not depart from it."* Of course, he then proceeds throughout the rest of the book to tell his son *the way he should go*, namely the path of wisdom. He also gives him a systematic approach to *train up a child*.

Because of the alarming numbers of young people in our time that grow up in a "Christian home" and yet turn away from the faith as teens, many have imagined that Proverbs 22:6 is not as didactic as it appears. They have imagined that there is no promise from God that if we follow his Word in training our children, they will stay true to him in adulthood and not rebel. However, we are convinced that if we interpret this verse in the context of the entire book of Proverbs and, yes, the Bible, we will see that this is indeed a promise that our children will not turn from the way if we train them in God's way. In the next few chapters we will explore this systematic approach to training our children in the way they should go, but first let's look at the two possible results of our child rearing that Proverbs gives us: the triumph of raising wise children and the tragedy of raising fools.

I. Wise Children

Proverbs 15:20: *A wise son maketh a glad father: but a foolish man despiseth his mother.*

Proverbs 23:15: *My son, if thine heart be wise, my heart shall rejoice, even mine.*

Proverbs 23:24–25: *The father of the righteous shall greatly rejoice: and he that begetteth a wise child shall have joy of him. Thy father and thy mother shall be glad and she that bare thee shall rejoice.*

Proverbs 29:3: *Whoso loveth wisdom rejoiceth his father: but he that keepeth company with harlots spendeth his substance.*

Proverbs 27:11: *My son, be wise and make my heart glad, that I may answer him that reproacheth me.*

As we let the teachings of Proverbs saturate our souls, we will begin to realize that our goal is not only to raise children who are obedient but also ultimately to raise children who are wise. Here are just a few of the attributes of a wise child for us to consider:

• **Reveres God**

Proverbs 9:10: *The fear of the LORD is the beginning of wisdom: and the knowledge of the holy is understanding.*

• **Listens**

Proverbs 1:5: *A wise man will hear and will increase learning; and a man of understanding shall attain unto wise counsels:*

• **Diligent**

Proverbs 10:5: *He that gathereth in summer is a wise son: but he that sleepeth in harvest is a son that causeth shame.*

• **Obedient**

Proverbs 13:1: *A wise son heareth his father's instruction: but a scorner heareth not rebuke.*

• **Self-Controlled**

Proverbs 10:19: *In the multitude of words there wanteth not sin: but he that refraineth his lips is wise.*

• **Seeks Wise Friends**

Proverbs 13:20: *He that walketh with wise men shall be wise: but a companion of fools shall be destroyed.*

• **Humble**

Proverbs 11:2: *When pride cometh, then cometh shame: but with the lowly is wisdom.*

- **Gentle**

Proverbs 10:11: The mouth of a righteous man is a well of life: but violence covereth the mouth of the wicked.

- **Honest**

Proverbs 13:5: A righteous man hateth lying: but a wicked man is loathsome and cometh to shame.

The list could go on and on. As fathers and mothers, we need to dig into Proverbs and find out what God says a wise and righteous child is like. In the New Testament we need to study the epistles, where over and over the Apostle Paul lists the fruit of the Spirit. Then we need to diligently train these traits into our children.

II. Foolish Children

Proverbs 17:25: A foolish son is a grief to his father and bitterness to her that bare him.

Proverbs 10:1: The proverbs of Solomon. A wise son maketh a glad father: but a foolish son is the heaviness of his mother.

Proverbs 15:20: A wise son maketh a glad father: but a foolish man despiseth his mother.

Proverbs 17:21: He that begetteth a fool doeth it to his sorrow: and the father of a fool hath no joy.

Proverbs 19:13: A foolish son is the calamity of his father: and the contentions of a wife are a continual dropping.

The other end of the spectrum is the fool. As we progress into the how-to of raising a wise child, we will see that there is no effort required in raising a fool. All children, if not trained, will automatically become fools by default.

Proverbs 29:15: The rod and reproof give wisdom: but a child left to himself bringeth his mother to shame.

To the degree that we as parents, by faith, are diligent in training our children, they will become wiser and more fertile soil for God's Spirit to do his work. To the degree that we shirk our duty to train our children and instead allow their friends and the culture to train them, they will become more foolish and hardened.

Proverbs 22:15: Foolishness is bound in the heart of a child; but the rod of correction shall drive it far from him.

Again, here are just a few attributes of the foolish child for us to consider.

- **Disobedient and Rebellious**

Proverbs 15:5: *A fool despiseth his father's instruction: but he that regardeth reproof is prudent.*

- **Self-Centered**

Proverbs 18:2: *A fool hath no delight in understanding, but that his heart may discover itself.*

- **Talks Back**

Proverbs 18:6: *A fool's lips enter into contention and his mouth calleth for strokes.*

- **Fights and Argues**

Proverbs 20:3: *It is an honour for a man to cease from strife: but every fool will be meddling.*

- **Lying**

Proverbs 10:18: *He that hideth hatred with lying lips and he that uttereth a slander, is a fool.*

- **Anger and Discontentment**

Proverbs 12:16: *A fool's wrath is presently known: but a prudent man covereth shame.*

- **Disrupts the Home**

Proverbs 11:29: *He that troubleth his own house shall inherit the wind: and the fool shall be servant to the wise of heart.*

- **Mischievous and Unkind**

Proverbs 10:23: *It is as sport to a fool to do mischief: but a man of understanding hath wisdom.*

- **Proud**

Proverbs 12:15: *The way of a fool is right in his own eyes: but he that hearkeneth unto counsel is wise.*

- **Stubborn**

Proverbs 17:10: *A reproof entereth more into a wise man than an hundred stripes into a fool.*

- **Self-Absorbed**

Proverbs 28:26: *He that trusteth in his own heart is a fool: but whoso walketh wisely, he shall be delivered.*

- **Self-Indulged and Lazy**

Proverbs 10:5: *He that gathereth in summer is a wise son: but he that sleepeth in harvest is a son that causeth shame.*

We can see how this again coincides with the epistles where Paul lists the works of the flesh, especially Galatians 5:19–21:

Now the works of the flesh are manifest, which are these; Adultery, fornication, uncleanness, lasciviousness, Idolatry, witchcraft, hatred, variance, emulations, wrath, strife, seditions, heresies, envyings, murders, drunkenness, revellings, and such like: of the which I tell you before, as I have also told you in time past, that they which do such things shall not inherit the kingdom of God.

The Injury of Indulgence

If we boil down the various characteristics of the fool found in Proverbs, we discover a glaring common denominator: selfishness. There is a destructive trend today in our society regarding parenting that has been perpetrated on us by the evolutionary child psychologists and secular humanists in our public education system. This philosophy has been the cause of two or three generations of some of the biggest fools in modern history. This trend is that the ultimate goal of parenting is to have happy children. To achieve this aim, parents indulge their children's every want and desire in a vain effort to keep them amused. If at any time the child is discontent, the parent is to snap to and throw everything in the book at the child until they are satisfied once again. This is no more clearly illustrated than by a walk through a grocery store. We see harried moms with their little masters proclaiming loudly and pointing to the object of their latest desire. If the child is not immediately gratified, he proceeds to make the mother's world absolutely miserable until she gives in to his demands. Instead of succumbing to their extortion, we are to by outward constraint control them and eventually teach them to control themselves.

Romans 13:14: *But put ye on the Lord Jesus Christ and make not provision for the flesh, to fulfil the lusts thereof.*

All children are born completely selfish and programmed to fulfill the needs of their flesh. For the first few months of that baby's life, all it knows is eating and sleep. Its every thought is its comfort: *I'm hungry, I want to be held, I'm dirty, I'm wet, I'm bored,* and so on. If it isn't instantly gratified, it cries until its wishes are fulfilled. As far as that child is concerned, the whole world revolves around him. Some of you are saying to yourselves, "This sounds like my sixteen-year-old." This is all normal and healthy for a BABY! But as that baby gets older, at least by six months, Dad and Mom are supposed to start teaching him restraint and the beginning steps of self-control. By the time he is twelve months old, he should know that when Dad or Mom speaks, he is expected to instantly obey and that there will be consequences if he does not. By the time he is five years of age, he should be completely self-controlled and in total subjection to his parents. From age five to twenty, 90 percent of his training should be internal, conforming his heart and mind to the Word of God. This was the absolute norm for children a hundred years ago. However, after the rise of modern child psychology, which is grounded in evolutionary theory, parents began to be told that their children's happiness was the primary concern of child rearing. This ideology can be seen in the propaganda of everything from children's cereal commercials on TV to children's books and films. Secular child-rearing books in the 1960s told parents that children had rights and that parents should negotiate with their kids. They postulated that authoritarian control and corporal punishment were old-fashioned ideas and damaging to a child's psyche. The evolutionists propagated such myths as that of children going through stages like the "terrible twos" and rebelling in adolescence because they imagined that it followed their models of evolutionary growth. To them, the terrible twos represented the cavemen/Neanderthal type and so on. The basis for much of this was the rise of moral relativism. Under this teaching there is no absolute truth in the world, so morality is relevant to whatever situation you find yourself in. Parents were told that they shouldn't force their views and values on their children but should instead let them be creative and decide for themselves such important issues as religion, faith, and behavior. The results have been a few generations of selfish, self-indulged, self-absorbed people who are like the baby whose only goal in life is to be made happy and comfortable, but they are not nearly as cute and cuddly as the baby.

The Bible never commands us to make our children happy. It does command us to bring them up in the nurture (loving and cherishing) and admonition (correction and instruction) of the Lord. In fact, it teaches us that some of the time we are to make our children very unhappy.

Hebrews 12:11: *Now no chastening for the present seemeth to be joyous, but grievous: nevertheless afterward it yieldeth the peaceable fruit of righteousness unto them which are exercised thereby.*

The Bible gives us a much different picture as it talks about learning to suffer gracefully and denying ourselves and making no provision for our flesh.

We never allowed whining in our home. We went out of our way to show our children that they were not the center of the universe. The world did not exist to gratify them; on the contrary, they were on this earth for a purpose. God put them here for a reason. He has a mission for them, and it is not to indulge in sensual pleasure the rest of their lives.

The truth is, the great majority of Christian parents have bought into the lie that successful child rearing is "keeping your children happy." Consequently, we give to them and do for them and consult them about their feelings until they get the idea that the world does revolve around them, that their happiness is paramount, that we will take care of them until they leave college, that after that some corporation will take care of them or the government will, and if at any time during this process they get unhappy with anything, they can sue somebody because of it. Children who are constantly and boldly expressing their wants about everything are self-indulged. Every time we hear a child whine, "I want so and so" or "I don't like such and such," it makes us want to tell the poor child, "No one cares what you want and no one cares what you like or don't like." The sad thing is that his little momma and daddy have demonstrated to him over and over that his wants do take priority, and that is why he feels so free in expressing them.

Parents often disguise their lack of will and courage to train their children biblically as "love." But the truth is that they are doing eternal damage to their child, and that cannot be defined as love. Because, when that child grows up, his self-absorption and lack of obedience to his parents will transfer to his self-will and lack of obedience to God, which has eternal consequences.

The saddest part is that these children are the most miserable, ungrateful, selfish, angry, unhappy, discontent people in the world, and the reward that their parents get for indulging them is that the parents get disrespected, ridiculed, disregarded, and ultimately rejected.

God's plan is for parents to train out the foolishness and selfishness in their children through outward constraints until the child can control himself. At that point, as we have said, the training turns mostly inward and becomes *discipleship*.

Parents, we must repent of our own selfishness, laziness, self-indulgence, and self-absorption and we must determine to control our children outwardly through training and discipline until they mature enough to exercise restraint and self-control on their own, or we can be guaranteed to produce a house full of "fools."

Thankfully, God has given us in the book of Proverbs the how-to of raising a wise child and also how to avoid raising a fool.

Proverbs 29:15: *The rod and reproof give wisdom: but a child left to himself bringeth his mother to shame.*

Proverbs 22:15: *Foolishness is bound in the heart of a child; but the rod of correction shall drive it far from him.*

The word here in Proverbs 22:15 translated as *foolishness* is the Hebrew word *ivveleth*. It is used only twenty-five times in the Bible, and all of them are in Proverbs with the exception of one occurrence in Psalms 69:5. The *Strong's Hebrew Dictionary* and the *Brown, Driver, Briggs Hebrew Dictionary* both say that *ivveleth* means literally *foolishness or the state of being a fool*. If we look at those twenty-five places in the Bible where *ivveleth* is used, it is very clear that it means those traits of a fool that we looked at above. So Proverbs 22:15 is telling us that the way to have wise children and not fools is to drive the foolishness out of them with a rod.

In the next chapter we will delve into the issues of training wisdom into our children and training foolishness out. As we are obedient to his Word, God works with us and through us and in our children to bring about the transformation from fools to wise men.

The Truth of Training

✦

(This discussion is only a brief summary of the concept of child training and is not intended to be an exhaustive work on the subject. For further study, the authors would implore you to acquire and study three books: *What the Bible Says About Child Training* by Richard Fugate, *To Train Up a Child* by Michael and Debbie Pearl, and *Child Training Tips* by Reb Bradley. These three authors have many other books, tapes, and videos that have also been invaluable to the Bullen family.)

Proverbs 22:6
Train up a child in the way he should go: and when he is old, he will not depart from it.

One of the tragedies that has resulted from these modern trends in child rearing is that children are no longer being trained to become adults. No longer is childhood the training ground for future adulthood. Instead, childhood has evolved into some mystical phase where the child indulges in endless pleasure with no responsibility and very little boundaries. Of course, the child best be sure they stay within the boundaries of what will not enrage their beleaguered parents, who have themselves begrudgingly left the mystical phase of childhood behind and are now burdened with the responsibility of adulthood. The goal is no longer to use those years to teach and prepare children to be useful, mature members of society and the kingdom of God. Rather, we try to extend this self-indulgent phase as long as possible (at least through college) and, like Peter Pan, we try to never grow up. Those who have given in and "grown up" often turn back and attempt to relive the phase vicariously through their own children.

We have gotten away from training children to be what they should be. We have abdicated our responsibility to *train* them to be obedient, kind, loving, respectful, helpful, courteous, diligent, dependable, honest, chivalric, ladylike, gentle, strong, and so on. We have left it up to the pastor, the youth pastor, the

52

Sunday school teacher, the Christian school, or—worse yet—the public school. Actually, in our neglect of our responsibility to guide them, we have unintentionally left it up to their own self-will and their peers to train them. In our discussion of the "value of a vision," we challenged you to have a dream for your sons and daughters. The way that you achieve that dream is by training.

Just as a drill sergeant trains his troops through six weeks of seemingly endless drills and marches before they are ready for battle, so we can train our "recruits" to be soldiers for Christ. The sergeant has only six weeks, or thirteen weeks for marines; we have twenty years. If a coach can turn a group of rowdy athletes into a championship team through consistent and persistent training, instruction, and practice, we can certainly, through God's Spirit and his Word, turn our family into a championship team for the kingdom of God. The teaching and training of the sergeant and the coach are very deliberate and intentional with a certain outcome in mind. However, in our thinking we often expect our children to just "pick up" our values along the way. We find so many parents subscribing to a "Christianized" version of this error. They mistakenly assume that maturity and responsibility in a child automatically coincides with his getting older. They somehow think that children will absorb certain virtues and will be kind, giving, loving, serving, and mannerly just because they are in church on Sunday or they go to a Christian school. If they see a child who is mature for his age and has his parents' values and morals, they somehow feel that it must have something to do with his temperament or personality.

The parents who have swallowed this philosophy, constantly exhibit their belief in it by becoming angry with their children for doing things that to the parents are obviously wrong but of which the children seem to be totally oblivious. But have they ever intentionally trained them in that specific behavior?

Sometimes we try to discipline up a child in the way he should go. Or we try to punish up a child in the way he should go. We leave them to themselves for the most part, expecting that they should know what is right and wrong, and then we periodically step in (when we can't take it anymore) and "correct" them. Then we wonder why they don't delight in us and want to be around us and why they don't find joy in our presence.

Imagine a sergeant who sent his recruits directly into battle without the benefit of "boot camp" and then was surprised when they did not succeed, or a coach who expected to have a championship team without scheduling practices.

Or a coach or sergeant who thought that his players or soldiers would just "pick up on" the things that were necessary to win or survive as they went along, and if necessary he would correct their errors as they arose. It would be chaos.

The vain philosophies of the world have gotten us so turned around that we train our pets better than we train our kids. We are not surprised when we see animals, who are not made in the image of God, trained to do all kinds of incredible things, and yet we are amazed that someone could train a two-year-old, who is vastly more intelligent than any animal, to behave all the time and be happy and contented. The truth is that a child can be trained to be whatever we want him to be. This is why we started this book out with a discussion on the "Value of a Vision" because we can shape our children, through training, into greatness, mediocrity, or evil; it is in our hands. We either train them by diligent effort to obey God's word or train them to live by their natural lusts and desires through default and neglect. Make no mistake about it. All children are trained. If we don't like what they have become, we must admit our guilt and change our training.

How do we get our children to listen and obey the first time without fail? The same way a terrorist organization gets a young man or woman to strap on a bomb and blow themselves and everyone around them to kingdom come: training and instruction.

How does that lion tamer at the circus get the "king of beasts" to obey his every whim? Training and instruction. How do we get a two-year-old to obey instantly, stop whining, or sit quietly in church? It is as simple as using a miniature version of that lion tamer's whip, something our grandmothers called a switch and the book of Proverbs calls a rod. The lion tamer doesn't use the whip to punish or discipline the lion but to train him to obey. Neither does he wait until they are in the center ring at the circus before he trains the lion. He trains him patiently and diligently behind the scenes so that when they enter the ring both know their place; they both know who the trainer is, who is the trainee is, and what is expected of each.

For instance, if we want to train our sons (who are already in subjection to our authority) how to respond when introduced to an adult, we simply have a training session where we go through the steps: "OK, son, first you look them in the eye and smile, and then you extend your hand and give them a firm handshake and say, 'Nice to meet you, Mr. Jones.'" We then practice it several times until they have it down. Next, make it a point to introduce them to several adult acquaintances over the next few weeks and then reinforce and offer suggestions as necessary until they have mastered that skill.

Any social skill, virtue, or good behavior can be trained into a child in the same manner once you have trained out the foolishness and have their obedience and respect. Training a two-year-old to sit quietly in church (not that this is a great moral matter, but it is indicative of a deeper issue, namely, who is in charge, the God-ordained authority or the child) is as simple as training him to sit quietly, at your command, in his high chair during the week.

Lisa used to have a little rod (the little plastic rod that we turn to open and close our mini-blinds) with her constantly when our children were small. When they would start to fuss or kick on the diaper-changing table or in the high chair, she would say "no" in a normal but firm voice; if the baby didn't instantly stop, she would give him a little pop on the bare leg with the rod. The baby would come to associate the slight pain on the leg with the word "no."

She was very consistent with this and would escalate it, as necessary, until the child yielded. Before long she would just say "no" in a normal but authoritative voice and the baby would instantly comply. Then, if we were in church and the child started to fuss or wiggle, she would simply say "no" again in a normal tone of voice and the baby would be still. Sometimes she would have to pull the rod out of the diaper bag and show it to the baby and the struggle was over.

The baby had learned that Momma is in charge and that submission of his will to her is much less painful than persisting in getting his own way. This was not punishment because with our children we used this from six months on; they were too young to even know about rules and such. We were simply helping them, by using outward constraint, to deny their natural tendency to indulge their flesh, and we were planting the seeds of self-discipline, which would someday make them fertile soil for the Spirit of God to train and instruct them in his law.

If Matthew was present, he would reinforce this and would likewise train the children. Most people wait until the child is totally out of control before they resort to the use of the rod. Although this can work if they are consistent and firm enough, that type of correction is reactive whereas training is proactive and dramatically more effective.

Training is preventative. Correction is curative. Remember, "An ounce of prevention…" Of course, there were always some "spineless" moms and dads who thought we were cruel for spanking a baby but who envied the peace and harmony that our home experienced. There were also those who were amazed that we were so "lucky" as to have five children who were born with such perfect temperaments. We like how Johnnie Seago, our pastor's wife, responds to that kind of remark: "Yes, and I have found that the harder I work, the 'luckier' I get."

Sadly, these folks were ignorant of the Bible or were not willing to trust God's word in this area, and for most of them the results have been tragic. Older children can be trained even if they have not had the benefit of being trained from the time they were babies as we have suggested. First, the parent must confess their sin and ask forgiveness of their child for not training them and for allowing them to persist in their pursuit of self-indulgence. Next, they must begin to consistently correct and train until the child realizes that Dad and Mom are serious and that it is futile to resist, and then they will submit. Sadly, most modern parents are so self-indulged themselves that they are unwilling to stay the course and put in the effort to train their children.

Children are longing to be led, they are miserable in their sin, and they instinctively feel the need to be controlled. The most unhappy youths in the world are the ones who are the least disciplined. Have you ever seen a happy, contented, joyful brat? No! They are sour, complaining, moaning, groaning, manipulative, whining wretches. They are just trying to tell us that they need to be controlled and they can't do it themselves. That's why God gave them parents.

As we have said, there are wonderful books out there that go into great detail on the philosophy and methodology of training, so our purpose here is not to write an exhaustive work on the subject but to introduce God's systematic plan of child training and to whet the appetite of parents to search out and discover the truths of training that have been such a blessing to us.

As we discussed in the last chapter, the goal of our child rearing is to have wise children. Below is the systematic plan that Proverbs gives us for training up our child "in the way he should go"

Training
I. Grant Love and Acceptance, Age 0–100 (Build relationship/win the heart)

Proverbs 4:3–4: For I was my father's son, tender and only beloved in the sight of my mother. He taught me also, and said unto me, Let thine heart retain my words: keep my commandments, and live.

Proverbs 17:6: Children's children are the crown of old men; and the glory of children are their fathers.

Proverbs 20:7: The just man walketh in his integrity: his children are blessed after him.

Proverbs 15:17: Better is a dinner of herbs where love is, than a stalled ox and hatred therewith.

Proverbs 16:24: Pleasant words are as an honeycomb, sweet to the soul, and health to the bones.

Proverbs 22:1: A good name is rather to be chosen than great riches, and loving favour rather than silver and gold.

For every negative word we say to our children, we should say twenty positive words. We must spend time with them enjoying the things they enjoy, laughing, playing, and having fun together. Then when we correct them they will receive it so much better because they are fully secure in our love for them. It is hard to rebel against your best friend. By that, we don't mean that parents should lower themselves to try and be their child's peer. Rather they should build a close adult–child friendship. If you have a deep and enjoyable relationship with your child, there will be much less need for correction because your child will not want to break fellowship with you. When you do have to correct them, it will be much more effectual.

II. Gain Obedience, Age 0–6 (Drive away the foolishness/train proper behavior)

Proverbs 29:15: The rod and reproof give wisdom: but a child left to himself bringeth his mother to shame.

Proverbs 22:15: Foolishness is bound in the heart of a child; but the rod of correction shall drive it far from him.

Proverbs 13:24: He that spareth his rod hateth his son: but he that loveth him chasteneth him betimes.

Proverbs 19:18: Chasten thy son while there is hope, and let not thy soul spare for his crying.

Proverbs 23:13–14: Withhold not correction from the child: for if thou beatest him with the rod, he shall not die. Thou shalt beat him with the rod, and shalt deliver his soul from hell.

Proverbs 3:12: For whom the LORD loveth he correcteth; even as a father the son in whom he delighteth.

Proverbs 29:17: Correct thy son, and he shall give thee rest; yea, he shall give delight unto thy soul.

Proverbs 20:30: The blueness of a wound cleanseth away evil: so do stripes the inward parts of the belly.

Proverbs 10:13: In the lips of him that hath understanding wisdom is found: but a rod is for the back of him that is void of understanding.

Proverbs 26:3: A whip for the horse, a bridle for the ass, and a rod for the fool's back.

Proverbs 19:29: Judgments are prepared for scorners, and stripes for the back of fools.

Once we have brought our children's will into total subjection to our authority through love, example, and training/correction, then and only then are we able to effectively instruct and teach them virtue, values, and godly character.

Sadly, so often we see young parents (especially homeschoolers) trying to teach and instruct their children without first getting them under control. Nothing is more frustrating or more useless.

There have been times in our family's life when we felt that our children were getting out of control and that there was a spirit of rebellion beginning to brew. Harmony, love, and peace were beginning to wane in our home. We would immediately shut down all activities in the family, including sports, school, extra-curricular activities, all socializing, and sometimes even church, for a period of a few days or even weeks and we would refocus on loving each other, training, and correction until they were back in total subjection and willing obedience to their God-ordained authorities, Mom and Dad. We dubbed this time "family building."

Our friends and our church knew that when they didn't see or hear from us for a season that the Bullens were family building again. When we felt that things were back in order, we would begin to add activities back into our family life. At this point our children were ready to again receive instruction and teaching.

III. Give Instruction, Age 6–12 (Pour in the word of wisdom/teach them the "why" of obedience)

Proverbs 1:8: My son, hear the instruction of thy father, and forsake not the law of thy mother:

Proverbs 2:1: My son, if thou wilt receive my words, and hide my commandments with thee;

Proverbs 3:1: My son, forget not my law; but let thine heart keep my commandments:

Proverbs 4:1–4: Hear, ye children, the instruction of a father, and attend to know understanding. For I give you good doctrine, forsake ye not my law. For I was my father's son, tender and only beloved in the sight of my mother. He taught me also, and said unto me, Let thine heart retain my words: keep my commandments, and live.

Proverbs 4:11: I have taught thee in the way of wisdom; I have led thee in right paths.

Proverbs 4:20: My son, attend to my words; incline thine ear unto my sayings.

Proverbs 5:1: My son, attend unto my wisdom, and bow thine ear to my understanding:

Proverbs 6:20: My son, keep thy father's commandment, and forsake not the law of thy mother:

Proverbs 7:1–4: My son, keep my words, and lay up my commandments with thee. Keep my commandments, and live; and my law as the apple of thine eye. Bind them upon thy fingers, write them upon the table of thine heart. Say unto wisdom, Thou art my sister; and call understanding thy kinswoman:

Proverbs 8:32: Now therefore hearken unto me, O ye children: for blessed are they that keep my ways.

Proverbs 8:33: Hear instruction, and be wise, and refuse it not.

Proverbs 13:1: A wise son heareth his fathers instruction: but a scorner heareth not rebuke.

Proverbs 15:5: A fool despiseth his father's instruction: but he that regardeth reproof is prudent.

Proverbs 23:22: Hearken unto thy father that begat thee, and despise not thy mother when she is old.

Parents, douse your children's hearts and minds with the Word of God. Teach them. Catechize them. Instruct them in the what and why of your values, beliefs, and principles. This is the time to provide them with the facts. Later, as we will see below, you will coach and counsel them to develop that information into principles by which to live, also known as wisdom.

IV. Guide by Mentorship, Age 12–18 (Coaching)

Proverbs 23:26: My son, give me thine heart, and let thine eyes observe my ways.

Proverbs 11:14: Where no counsel is, the people fall: but in the multitude of counsellors there is safety.

Proverbs 12:15: The way of a fool is right in his own eyes: but he that hearkeneth unto counsel is wise.

Proverbs 15:22: Without counsel purposes are disappointed: but in the multitude of counsellors they are established.

Proverbs 19:20: Hear counsel, and receive instruction, that thou mayest be wise in thy latter end.

Proverbs 20:18: Every purpose is established by counsel: and with good advice make war.

Proverbs 24:6: For by wise counsel thou shalt make thy war: and in multitude of counsellors there is safety.

Proverbs 27:9: Ointment and perfume rejoice the heart: so doth the sweetness of a man's friend by hearty counsel.

This is an extremely joyful and rewarding time when you begin to relate to your children as adults and no longer as children. By now you have built an unbreakable bond of mutual respect, love, and affection with your child. You have subjected their will to yours through biblical training and correction. You have thoroughly taught, instructed, and catechized them in truth. Now you are ready to come alongside them as a friend, counselor, coach, and mentor and teach them how to use the knowledge that you have given them to become the man or woman God desires for them to be. These stages will often overlap one another. There will be regressions and gaps that need to be filled in, but the general focus and mode of your parenting during these stages should follow these points and the joy of the triumph will be yours.

The Challenge of Consistency

✦

1 Corinthians 15:58
Therefore, my beloved brethren, be ye stedfast, unmoveable, always abounding in the work of the Lord, forasmuch as ye know that your labour is not in vain in the Lord.

In order to maximize the benefits of our training and instruction, we must strive to be consistent. One mistake that many parents make is that they are very firm in one instance and then lenient in another concerning the same issue. Many times we feel we are too busy, too distracted, or too weary to stop and deal directly with a situation of training or discipline and so we "let it go" this time. But at other times we are inspired and recommitted to proper discipline in our home and so we overreact or at least act more stringently than we have at other times. Even worse, we respond one way in public (where we are embarrassed by our children's misbehavior) and another way at home (where no one knows the difference). What we are actually doing is training our kids that Dad and Mom don't really know what is good or bad, important or not so important, and that we are merely flying by the seat of our pants. This can be a grievous source of confusion and frustration for our children and will eventually lead to their disregarding us completely because we are no longer credible as authorities.

Ephesians 6:4: *And, ye fathers, provoke not your children to wrath: but bring them up in the nurture and admonition of the Lord.*

So often we have seen parents who, depending on their mood at the time, correct very sternly or don't correct at all for the exact same infraction. Nothing will provoke a child quicker than not knowing what to expect and when to expect it. We also have to be careful to keep our word. Many times we threaten punishment that we really don't have the will to enforce. This is damaging. It would be better, though not ideal, to *not* take a stand on an issue than to take a stand and then not follow through. We shouldn't tell our children that they will get a spanking if they do a certain thing unless we are prepared to give them the spank-

61

ing. If we threaten and then don't follow through, we become like the little boy in classic literature who "cried wolf" one too many times. Eventually our children will tune out our words as simple background noise and irrelevant chatter. We as parents should attempt to be very predictable. Our children should know that if they behave in a certain manner, they can expect certain results, either positive or negative.

To do this, we must start by identifying, from the scriptures, our family's standards of conduct and the consequences of failure to meet these standards. Then we must clearly teach these rules and expectations to our children and establish corresponding penalties for not obeying them. For instance, we might have the following chart on the wall:

1. Failure to obey immediately when spoken to: 1 swat

2. Complaining or whining: 2 swats

3. Arguing and fussing: 5 swats

4. Lying: 15 swats

The secret at this point is to discipline ourselves to act consistently when these standards are broken. Many times young parents tell us, "If I followed this and was consistent, all I would do all day is carry a rod around and swat kids." EXACTLY!!! But, if you were consistent, you would only have to do so for about three days and then they would get the hint that Momma was serious and they would amend their behavior. From then on, life could return to normal with only one or two instances a day of consistently reinforcing the standard until eventually correction is rarely even needed. There would be no need for shouting, nagging, manipulating, promising, or threatening. Momma merely commands in a mild, relaxed tone, and if she is not instantly and unquestioningly obeyed, she simply swats the child firmly on the legs with the switch and then calmly repeats the command and, if necessary, swats until the desired result is achieved.
Proverbs 23:14: *Thou shalt beat him with the rod and shalt deliver his soul from hell.*

If our children's eternal destiny is not worth three days or a week of focused, consistent correction to bring them into subjection once again to Dad and Mom, then we have no business being parents. The sad thing is that parents "try" the rod a couple of times, but not consistently over a period of time, and then conclude it doesn't work on "this particular child" and go off in search of some psychobabbler's creative method of discipline. Of course, these never work either because the problem is the parent's lack of steady application of the method and not the method itself.

We can even be consistent when a situation comes up that is not specifically addressed by our set standards of conduct. We simply determine if the action was loving (the law of love) or if it was foolishness (self-indulgence). Our children should know that foolishness (as defined in the book of Proverbs) will always result in the rod. This way, there are no loopholes or gray areas and we don't have to cover every type of misbehavior imaginable in our chart of rules.

Proverbs 22:15: *Foolishness is bound in the heart of a child; but the rod of correction shall drive it far from him.*

The Bible says the rod of correction will drive it far from him. It doesn't say that "time-outs," or counting to 50,000, or jumping jacks, or standing in the corner, or grounding, or loss of privileges, or nagging, or manipulating, or berating, or coercing, or extorting, or bribing, or screaming, or negotiating, or pleading, or added chores, or any number of other forms of "creative discipline" will drive away the foolishness. It says the rod will. We should turn to it first rather than last when all else has failed and we are finally angry enough. Parents, quit frustrating your child with these silly, ineffectual practices and cleanse their hearts, minds, and consciences with a good spanking! The foolishness will flee and wisdom will grow in its place.

Father and mother, establish from scripture a clearly defined standard of behavior for your children and then consistently instruct and correct them accordingly and your children will be obedient, secure, relaxed, and contented and will bless all who know them.

The Endeavor of Education

✦

Psalm 78:1–7
<Maschil of Asaph.> Give ear, O my people, to my law: incline your ears to the words of my mouth. I will open my mouth in a parable: I will utter dark sayings of old: Which we have heard and known and our fathers have told us. We will not hide them from their children, shewing to the generation to come the praises of the LORD and his strength and his wonderful works that he hath done. For he established a testimony in Jacob and appointed a law in Israel, which he commanded our fathers, that they should make them known to their children: That the generation to come might know them, even the children which should be born; who should arise and declare them to their children: That they might set their hope in God and not forget the works of God, but keep his commandments:

In the passage above, Asaph reminds Israel that the responsibility of educating the next generation falls squarely on the shoulders of the fathers. He reminds them that in Deuteronomy 6:7–9 and 4:9–10 the Lord had commanded the fathers to teach their children and, through them, their children's children.

Deuteronomy 6:6–9: *And these words, which I command thee this day, shall be in thine heart: And thou shalt teach them* **<u>diligently</u>** *unto thy children and shalt talk of them when thou sittest in thine house and when thou walkest by the way and when thou liest down and when thou risest up. And thou shalt bind them for a sign upon thine hand and they shall be as frontlets between thine eyes. And thou shalt write them upon the posts of thy house and on thy gates.*

Asaph says that they will not hide the parables and dark sayings of old from their children. They will not hide the wisdom and knowledge of the ancients from their children.

Deuteronomy 4:9–10: *Only take heed to thyself and keep thy soul* **<u>diligently</u>***, lest thou forget the things which thine eyes have seen and lest they depart from thy heart all the days of thy life: but teach them thy sons and thy sons' sons; Specially the day that* *thou stoodest before the LORD thy God in Horeb, when the LORD said unto me, Gather me the people together and I will make them hear my words, that they may learn to fear me all the days that they shall live upon the earth and that they may teach their children.*

It has only been in the last 150 years that the majority of fathers have abdicated their role as the primary educator of their children and have left it up to the government and the Sunday school to teach and instruct them. If we are to have a blessed family, the father must take back his God-ordained role as educator and instructor. He must take an active role in determining the content and quality of the material that they are to study and administrate when and how they are taught.

For our family, homeschooling was the only option. We believed that the untold future generations that would come from our union were much too important and valuable for us to allow someone else to shape our children's view of the world and to fill their heads and hearts with values and beliefs that were not our own. It is true that in this setting the mother will be the one who interacts primarily with the children in their schooling, but make no mistake about it, it is the father's full responsibility to educate the children. His wife is his helper in this endeavor.

He must be integrally involved in deciding what core curriculum will be used and what enrichment materials he and his wife feel would benefit their children the most in their journey to maturity and usefulness in the kingdom of God.

First and foremost, our children's education must begin with the Bible. It often astounds us to meet and talk to homeschool families who do not have a Bible curriculum or who do not at least make the Bible one of their core subjects that they study each day. What an incredible oversight if we believe that math, English, or science have any meaning or value outside of the context of knowing God.

Proverbs 1:7: *The fear of the LORD is the beginning of knowledge: but fools despise wisdom and instruction.*

Proverbs 9:10: *The fear of the LORD is the beginning of wisdom: and the knowledge of the holy is understanding.*

Another passage of which we should take notice is 2 Peter 1:5: *"And beside this, giving all **diligence,** add to your faith virtue; and to virtue knowledge."* In our schooling, knowledge should be diligently obtained, but only upon a foundation of faith and virtue. Because of this, in our home school for the last thirteen years we have started the day with the Word of God. Get a solid Bible study curriculum and take your children through the entire Bible over the years. Of course, you will start small when they are young and then get more advanced as their knowledge and abilities grow. Study major doctrines of the Bible and major themes and major characters. Read the Bible through every year. Get the Word into your children. Then upon that foundation you can teach them all of the knowledge of the ages. If we do not first lay a solid groundwork of faith and virtue, our education will be no better than that in the failed government school system.

Never use schooling as discipline. Try never to be frustrated or angry when they don't understand something. (We have certainly learned this one out of our failures.) Don't tie your self-image to their progress. If you lovingly persist, eventually the light will come on and they will learn more in one month than they have in the last two years. Be patient. Don't try to pick the fruit too early. Let them grow at their unique pace. Don't get caught up with grade levels and scores. Remember, you are not public schooling at home. You are homeschooling. Remember that some of the greatest education your children will receive cannot be found in books. It is learned by being with your family going and doing and enjoying God's world. When our family moved to the mountains of New Mexico, we took a whole year off from school and camped out on the property, cut trees, cleared the land, excavated and poured footings, built roads, put in a mobile home, landscaped, and generally spent hundreds of hours together experiencing real life. When the kids went back to their studies at the end of that year, not only were they not behind but they had jumped a year ahead. Their minds were more developed and mature. The schoolwork became much easier for them. The confidence that was built into them that year was invaluable.

Teach your children to read and then teach them to love reading. All of the knowledge that man has accumulated over the last six thousand years is written down in a book somewhere. Teach your child to learn and to love to learn and then watch them go! We have hundreds of books in our home, and now that our children are all teens, they are beginning to build their own libraries. Sometimes they will be reading four or five books at the same time. Most of them average a couple books a week. The boys have read every book on Christian manhood and leadership that we can get our hands on, and the girls have done the same with books on Christian womanhood.

Cast for them a vision of what God can do with them. Put the desire in their hearts to be a world-changer and reinforce the fact that to do so they must learn, learn, learn, and they will astound you with their hunger and desire for knowledge.

On the other hand, allow them to numb their minds with too much television and video games and too much leisure and self-indulgence and they, like the river, will seek the path of least resistance and disappoint you in the end. Dad and Mom, grasp the vision of what you are doing in your child's education. You are preparing the next leaders of the world. This is not about which phonics program to use or how to find the easiest and least painful new gimmick to use. It is about rising above the details and seeing the big picture and envisioning the final product.

Again, the Apostle says in 2 Peter 1:5 that we are to *diligently* add to our faith, virtue, and knowledge and the Lord says in Deuteronomy 6:7 that we are to *diligently* teach our children. Thus, diligence with a Biblical foundation is the prime ingredient to successful home education rather than the perfect curriculum, the consummate schedule, or the right approach.

The Importance of Identity

✦

Proverbs 22:1
A good name is rather to be chosen than great riches and loving favour rather than silver and gold.
Ecclesiastes 7:1
A good name is better than precious ointment...

One of the secrets of a blessed family that is nearest and dearest to our hearts is the concept of building a family identity. It is an idea that has been almost totally lost in our modern culture but was a central theme in cultures of the past. By family identity, we mean that the parents build a certain awe and respect around the family's name. In our family, for instance, the words "the Bullen family" have become nearly sacred and are spoken, even almost whispered, with reverence and veneration as well as with pride and confidence. We have deliberately constructed and cultivated this phenomenon, first as a means of providing a great sense of security, belonging, and unity for our children and second as a defense against the barrages of "peer pressure" and "the generation gap," which are so prevalent in our society today.

Once upon a time, a man's favor, fortune, and future were all inextricably linked to his family name and whether it was honorable or not. Look at Solomon's statements in the verses above regarding a "good name." In times past, a man would die before he would dare to, in some way, besmirch his family's good name. People were identified with their family line. Families had crests, and knights of old would proudly display these emblems on their armor and on the standards flying over their dwellings. People were distinguished as Matthew the son of Jack or as Luke of the house of Bullen. These were titles of great honor and pride.

Today in our culture it is exactly the opposite. Teenage boys and girls are ashamed of their old man and old lady. They are mortified if their peer group sees them with their parents, and heaven forbid if their little brother or sister is tagging along. They would die a thousand deaths before they would hug their mother in public or kiss their father in front of their friends. They would die ten thousand deaths before they would show public affection or be associated with a younger sibling. Instead their family is a target for mocking and making fun of. The all-important relationships in their lives are their friends at school or the church youth group, not the family that God ordained. This ought not to be and it is relatively simple to remedy.

Before we can teach our children to be proud to be a part of our family, we must be excited and proud of the family that God has given us. No matter what the past has been, we can determine right now, from this day forward, to lift up and honor in our heart and with our mouth the family and the family name that God has given us. We must start by lifting up our family before our children and the world around us as the marvelous gift from God that it is and be grateful for this blessing from heaven! We must explain to them the significance of the family in God's ultimate plan for the universe and help them to see what a privilege it is for them to be included in this majestic purpose.

Make your home a hallowed hall that stands to house this blessed family. Teach your children that the family is a picture of heaven on this earth and a reflection of the Godhead and of the relationship between Christ and the church. Impart to them a vision of how their behavior either enhances or hinders these depictions of spiritual things to a lost and dying world. They should know and feel that they are part of a fabulous quest to take dominion of the earth and to build God's kingdom in this world! They should see that their family is a grand experiment in living out the "Law of Love"! Show them how your family is God's building block of his church, the Christian community, and the kingdom of God!

Wives, we must build up our husbands to our children as the hero of our home. He is that knight in shining armor, bearing the herald of our family before him as he goes out to conquer the world for Christ. He is the king, the monarch, the emperor, the champion of the family name, the lord protector, and the loving guide of our castle.

Husbands, we must build up our wives before our children as the queen and treasure of our domain. They must know that we see her as a most precious jewel and the fair lady for whom we toil and do battle in the world. They must be charged with respecting and adoring her and assisting her in her tasks as gentlewoman of the realm.

We can do some research on our family name and teach its history to our children. We can find out our family crest and put one up on the wall. Let them know about those who have gone before and paved the way for them in this world. For instance, our children know that the name Bullen is Norman, from the French city of Boulogne. Our first ancestor in England, Count Eustace de Boulogne fought alongside William the Conqueror at the battle of Hastings in AD 1066. and that our first ancestor in America was Deacon Samuel Bullen, who came from England on the Speedwell in 1634, only fourteen years after the Pilgrims landed at Plymouth. Give them a sense of family history, even if it is only three or four generations back. Teach them that our Sovereign God in his Divine Providence has brought your family, as Mordecai told Esther, to the kingdom for such a time as this. Give them a sense of destiny.

We love to have family traditions that we observe at different times of the year or on special occasions. For instance, we love the Christmas season, and so years ago we started several family traditions such as baking cookies together, Dad and all, or caroling in our neighborhood every year or reading Charles Dickens' *A Christmas Carol* out loud every year and many, many others. We went back and studied the history of Christmas and its traditions as they evolved primarily from German Christians after the Reformation and were later introduced in England by Prince Albert after he married Queen Victoria. We have traditions when we are on vacation, and we remind each other of the good times we have had together and the shared joys and sorrows that have made us more than just a collection of people living together in the same house. We rejoice exceedingly in each other's success, and we comfort and cry together in each other's heartaches. We do lots of things together as a family. We have chosen not to get overly involved in activities or sports that split us up and take us away from each other. We have made this such a focus for so long that we hate to be apart, and we find that we enjoy our friends and activities much more when we are together as a family rather than separated.

The Bullen children have been indoctrinated in the value of family bonds and ties, and they are now part of the vision and as much a part of the mission as are we as parents! They realize that we are preparing, teaching, molding, shaping, training, and instructing not just them but the next ten generations of Bullens yet to be born! We are shaping the future of the world! When our children marry, those new husbands and new wives will become a part of this family identity and their families will become a part of ours, and the love and the power will flow into those families as well, strengthening all who are touched by it. Our children say that Dad will be like a godly version of Vito Corleone, the Godfather. We envision the children and grandchildren and great-grandchildren around a massive table enjoying one of our favorite Christmas traditions we learned from Bob Cratchet, Mr. Scrooge's bookkeeper, toasting the founder of the feast!

As a family, we stick together. The Bible says in Ecclesiastes 4:9–12:

Two are better than one; because they have a good reward for their labour. For if they fall, the one will lift up his fellow: but woe to him that is alone when he falleth; for he hath not another to help him up. Again, if two lie together, then they have heat: but how can one be warm alone? And if one prevail against him, two shall withstand him; and a threefold cord is not quickly broken.

We will fight for each other and would die for each other. Each of us knows that we may fight a little among ourselves once in awhile, but heaven forbid if anyone from the outside were to jump on one of us because they would have to fight all of us to the death. We all know that we have each other's back covered. We are a team! No one had better speak anything ill of one of us to another of us because we are one and we are "the Bullen family!" Do you see the value of this powerful family identity? No peer group, peer pressure, or generation gap has a chance against a family who views each other and our relationship as the height of all that is good in this world and as a little piece of heaven on the earth. Our children would never even consider rebelling and casting a dark shadow over the good name of their family. They realize that their behavior reflects on every other person in our home and that bringing themselves down brings us all down. We are bound together by God; we are in a pursuit of holiness and usefulness to the kingdom of God, and we will conquer together.

This concept is not a onetime training session and then you have it ever thereafter. It must be constantly cultivated, nourished, and built upon. Many times we begin to feel that it is slipping away and that we have been guilty of neglecting our identity, and so we will slow down or even stop all activities for a while and just work on our togetherness and unity. Family vacations are a great way to renew and refresh this as well.

Another tradition that we enjoy is going out for breakfast every Saturday morning. We love to sit around the breakfast table and talk about our dreams and about our future plans. We laugh and enjoy each other.

Many evenings, we will just sit around in our living room talking about our family and what God is doing in each of our hearts and lives. Sometimes we discuss doctrine or biblical truths that we have been meditating on. Spending these times together ties strings of fellowship to each of our hearts and rebuilds our family identity.

What's truly exciting—and we will cover this more in the chapter on "The Magnificence of Ministry"—is that we have a vision of exporting our family identity to other families and teaching them how to be proud of the team that God is building in them. Recently a young man whom we know was struggling with his parents' authority. We told him how proud we were of his family and how blessed he was to live in a family that God was using. We told him that he was our hero because he was going to be a mighty warrior someday for God as a result of the awesome family of which he was a part. We explained that we wished that we were more like them. His chest popped out and he stood a little taller, and ever since then when we compliment him on doing something good he exclaims, "Well, I am a Smith [not his real last name] after all!" As we said at the beginning, family identity is a wonderful "secret" that God is using mightily in our family.

The Attitude of Gratitude

✦

Colossians 3:15
And let the peace of God rule in your hearts, to the which also ye are called in one body; and be ye thankful.

One of the most attractive qualities in a person is gratitude. Everyone wants to be around someone who is contented and at peace. The individual who is thankful, enjoys their life, enjoys the blessings of God, and enjoys people will never lack for friends because their joy will overflow onto those around them. The person who practices gratitude will be such a person. The old adage about some people who always view the glass as half empty while others always view the glass as half full is a commentary on gratitude. Either we are grateful for what we have and consequently sweet and joyful or we are discontented with what God has given us and consequently bitter, complaining, and always wanting more. People who are always dissatisfied with their current situation miss all of the blessings of life. They live either in the past or in the future and rarely enjoy the moment. This is evil and is a stench in the nostrils of God.

Romans 1:21, 22: *Because that, when they knew God, they glorified him not as God, neither were thankful; but became vain in their imaginations and their foolish heart was darkened. Professing themselves to be wise, they became fools…*

Romans 1:24a: *Wherefore God also gave them up…*

Within a marriage, discontentment and ingratitude are the death knell to a happy union. No man alive can please a discontented and ungrateful woman. No woman alive can please a discontented and ungrateful man.

Within a family, gratitude is an absolute must. There can be no blessedness without gratitude! The father and mother of a blessed family must develop this character quality for themselves, and they must teach it and train it into their children. No one wants to be around a whining, demanding, selfish, ungrateful, discontented child. The Bible says children are a blessing from God, but it will be very difficult to convince anyone of this if the child does not have the attitude of gratitude.

There are some very practical ways that we can train this wonderful trait into our children. As in every other area of the Christian life, we start out by obeying in faith. What we mean by this is that we act grateful. We discipline ourselves to speak thankfulness. We teach our children to practice gratitude by an act of their will by faith regardless of how they feel. Then God allows our emotions to catch up and we actually feel the contentment in our hearts.

First, set an example by practicing gratitude at every available opportunity. Dads, always express thankfulness to your wife for dinner, washing your clothes, cleaning the house, and so on in the presence of your children. Moms, remind your children how hard Daddy works for the food that you are preparing and how grateful you are to have a man who provides for his family. Parents, constantly express gratitude to God for his blessings, and point out to your children all of the little things that God has done for you and for them. When you see a sunset or a wildflower or a bright blue sky, express thanks to God and teach your children to admire God for his gracious gifts. Focus on the good and, by faith, give the bad to the Lord.

Philippians 4:8: Finally, brethren, whatsoever things are true, whatsoever things are honest, whatsoever things are just, whatsoever things are pure, whatsoever things are lovely, whatsoever things are of good report; if there be any virtue and if there be any praise, think on these things.

Second, train your children to express thanks to those who bless them. It is not enough to merely have them say "thank you" when someone gives them something. We must use those opportunities to really focus on gratitude. Make it a big deal that someone took the time and had the thoughtfulness to bless the child with a gift. We have always made it a tradition that if someone gives our child a gift, they give them a big hug and squeeze their neck and say, "Thank you."

When our children were very young, we started this custom at Christmas. We had observed other children, who were not trained, tearing through presents, and as soon as they had finished opening one, they tossed it aside to grab the next one. We felt this was dishonoring the givers as well as the Lord and was a terrible representation of the reason for the season. Consequently, when our children came along, we made it a habit that after opening each gift they would run to the giver of that gift and hug their neck and say, "Thank you!" This became a tremendous blessing to all who were present and made Christmas for our family one of the sweetest days of the year. Grandparents, aunts, and uncles loved to give gifts to our children because of the joy they would receive from the blessing of thanksgiving that was heaped upon them by the children. Soon our children began to be more interested in giving to each other on Christmas morning than in opening their own gifts because they loved to see their sibling run to them, throw their arms around them, and show their gratitude. We have suggested this to many families since who were alarmed and disgusted at their own children's attitude toward receiving gifts, and they have unanimously reported back to us the blessing that it has brought to their holidays.

Third, banish all whining, complaining, griping, and voicing of discontent from your home. Lead your children to understand that these bad habits are simply not allowed and will be punishable by the rod. If a child in our home ever said at the dinner table, "I don't like this," they received a double portion and were made to eat all of it. If they didn't eat it for dinner, they received the rod and then ate it cold for breakfast the next morning, and if not then, for lunch and dinner and so on. We did this not because their health would be permanently damaged if they did not eat their green beans but because their soul would be permanently damaged if they were permitted to develop the habit of being ungrateful. It takes a parent only a few instances of this type of strength of purpose for the child to realize that expressions of ingratitude are not in their best interest.

It was a hard-and-fast rule, in our family, that if the children were with Mommy at the store and they asked for something and she said "no" or "we'll see," they were to ask that one time and then be quiet because if they asked twice they were guaranteed that heaven and earth would move before they would ever get it. We did this not because their desires were wrong but because we were teaching them to be content with their mother's decisions and provision and to be grateful for what they had and not dwell on what they did not have. If our child ever said, "I want that," they could be assured that there would be ice-skating on the lake of fire before they ever received it. However, if they said, "May I have this please?" they were rewarded if it was a wise choice to begin with. To us, these were not just mere expressions of old-fashioned etiquette and politeness; they were tools to shape our child's soul into something God could work through and use.

Philippians 4:11–13: *Not that I speak in respect of want: for I have learned, in whatsoever state I am, therewith to be content. I know both how to be abased and I know how to abound: every where and in all things I am instructed both to be full and to be hungry, both to abound and to suffer need. I can do all things through Christ which strengtheneth me.*

1 Timothy 6:8: *And having food and raiment let us be therewith content.*

Hebrews 13:5: Let your conversation be without covetousness; and be content with such things as ye have: for he hath said, I will never leave thee, nor forsake thee.

Psalms 100:4: Enter into his gates with thanksgiving and into his courts with praise: be thankful unto him and bless his name.

Psalms 50:14: Offer unto God thanksgiving; and pay thy vows unto the most High:

Colossians 2:6–7: As ye have therefore received Christ Jesus the Lord, so walk ye in him: Rooted and built up in him and stablished in the faith, as ye have been taught, abounding therein with thanksgiving.

Ephesians 5:1–4: Be ye therefore followers of God, as dear children; And walk in love, as Christ also hath loved us and hath given himself for us an offering and a sacrifice to God for a sweetsmelling savour. But fornication and all uncleanness, or covetousness, let it not be once named among you, as becometh saints; Neither filthiness, nor foolish talking, nor jesting, which are not convenient: but rather giving of thanks.

Ephesians 5:20: Giving thanks always for all things unto God and the Father in the name of our Lord Jesus Christ;

Colossians 3:17: And whatsoever ye do in word or deed, do all in the name of the Lord Jesus, giving thanks to God and the Father by him.

1 Thessalonians 5:18: In every thing give thanks: for this is the will of God in Christ Jesus concerning you.

It is almost humorous to us, and yet at the same time sad, when someone asks one of us how we are doing and we begin to tell of the blessings of God upon our family and they exclaim, "Wow, God really blesses you guys. You always have some good thing to say or tell about. I wish I was in your family." The truth is that we have the same heartaches, failures, disappointments, hurts, and setbacks as any other family; it is just that we try very hard never to let those negatives be the focus of our attention and thereby rob us of enjoying the wonders of God's goodness that are all around us! Develop the attitude of gratitude and you and your family will be filled with joy and will spread infectious delight to those around you for the glory of God.

The Taming of the Tongue

✦

Psalms 34:13
Keep thy tongue from evil and thy lips from speaking guile.

Woven throughout this book is this subject of taming the tongue, but this is such an important topic in the life of a blessed family that it bears exploring in a chapter of its own. We can literally build our family or tear it down with our words. We remember the day that our family was at a conference several years ago and the speaker was talking about the power of the tongue. At one point he said, "When you are tempted to say something that is not edifying or uplifting, just bite your tongue." Then he proceeded to explain to us that he meant for us to literally stick our tongue out and gently bite on it as a reminder to not allow corrupt communication to proceed out of our mouths. We took that message to heart, and for years after that we would literally "bite" our tongues when tempted to say something evil. This practice immediately produced a great transformation in our marriage and family. The tongue can be a very powerful tool for building the family, or it can be a menacing weapon to destroy it. Here are some thoughts that God has about the potency of the tongue.

Proverbs 18:21: *Death and life are in the power of the tongue: and they that love it shall eat the fruit thereof.*

James 3:5–8: *Even so the tongue is a little member and boasteth great things. Behold, how great a matter a little fire kindleth! And the tongue is a fire, a world of iniquity: so is the tongue among our members, that it defileth the whole body and setteth on fire the course of nature; and it is set on fire of hell. For every kind of beasts and of birds and of serpents and of things in the sea, is tamed and hath been tamed of mankind: But the tongue can no man tame; it is an unruly evil, full of deadly poison.*

The Word has much to say about the mouth of the wicked.

Proverbs 16:27: *An ungodly man diggeth up evil: and in his lips there is as a burning fire.*

Titus 1:10: For there are many unruly and vain talkers and deceivers, specially they of the circumcision: Whose mouths must be stopped, who subvert whole houses, teaching things which they ought not, for filthy lucre's sake.

James 1:26: If any man among you seem to be religious and bridleth not his tongue, but deceiveth his own heart, this man's religion is vain.

Psalms 52:2–5: Thy tongue deviseth mischiefs; like a sharp razor, working deceitfully. Thou lovest evil more than good; and lying rather than to speak righteousness. Selah. Thou lovest all devouring words, O thou deceitful tongue. God shall likewise destroy thee for ever, he shall take thee away and pluck thee out of thy dwelling place and root thee out of the land of the living. Selah.

Proverbs 11:11: By the blessing of the upright the city is exalted: but it is overthrown by the mouth of the wicked.

We are challenged, encouraged, and commanded to speak good things and guard against using our tongues for evil.

Proverbs 13:3: He that keepeth his mouth keepeth his life: but he that openeth wide his lips shall have destruction.

Proverbs 21:23: Whoso keepeth his mouth and his tongue keepeth his soul from troubles.

Proverbs 10:32: The lips of the righteous know what is acceptable: but the mouth of the wicked speaketh frowardness.

Proverbs 10:11: The mouth of a righteous man is a well of life: but violence covereth the mouth of the wicked.

Proverbs 10:19: In the multitude of words there wanteth not sin: but he that refraineth his lips is wise.

Colossians 4:6: Let your speech be alway with grace, seasoned with salt, that ye may know how ye ought to answer every man.

Matthew 12:36–37: But I say unto you, That every idle word that men shall speak, they shall give account thereof in the day of judgment. For by thy words thou shalt be justified and by thy words thou shalt be condemned.

1Peter 3:10: For he that will love life and see good days, let him refrain his tongue from evil and his lips that they speak no guile:

Proverbs 16:23–24: The heart of the wise teacheth his mouth and addeth learning to his lips. Pleasant words are as an honeycomb, sweet to the soul and health to the bones.

Proverbs 25:11–12: A word fitly spoken is like apples of gold in pictures of silver. As an earring of gold and an ornament of fine gold, so is a wise reprover upon an obedient ear.

Proverbs 15:4: *A wholesome tongue is a tree of life: but perverseness therein is a breach in the spirit.*

Titus 2:8: *Sound speech, that cannot be condemned; that he that is of the contrary part may be ashamed, having no evil thing to say of you.*

The Apostle Paul gives us in Ephesians a very clear command regarding our tongues.

Ephesians 4:29–32: *Let no corrupt communication proceed out of your mouth, but that which is good to the use of edifying, that it may minister grace unto the hearers. And grieve not the holy Spirit of God, whereby ye are sealed unto the day of redemption. Let all bitterness and wrath and anger and clamour and evil speaking, be put away from you, with all malice: And be ye kind one to another, tenderhearted, forgiving one another, even as God for Christ's sake hath forgiven you.*

This is another great "secret" to having a blessed family. We must learn to use the power of our tongues to form our children and our spouses and to shape our brothers and sisters in Christ. We must learn to bless and not to curse, to compliment and not to condemn, to encourage and not to complain, to build up and not to tear down.

May this be our prayer:

Psalms 141:3: *Set a watch, O LORD, before my mouth; keep the door of my lips.*

The Haven of Harmony

✦

Proverbs 17:1

Better is a dry morsel and quietness therewith, than an house full of sacrifices with strife.

Psalms 133:1

<A Song of degrees of David.> Behold, how good and how pleasant it is for brethren to dwell together in unity!

How sweet and pleasant it is to live in a home that is a haven of harmony. Contrariwise, how annoying, irritating, and unpleasant it is to live in a home where there is fighting, arguing, strife, and disagreement.

Psalms 119:165: Great peace have they which love thy law: and nothing shall offend them.

Many years ago we determined before God that we would have a home that was a place of harmony, kindness, joy, and peace. We wanted our home to be a refuge from the cold, cruel world. Our desire was that when anyone entered our home they would immediately be struck by the peace of Christ that resided therein. We wished for an abode that was a proper representation of heaven on earth. We envisioned a place where the theme of the people who dwelt therein would be love and where Ephesians 4:32—*"And be ye kind one to another, tenderhearted, forgiving one another, even as God for Christ's sake hath forgiven you"*—would be their motto. We of course used many of the ideas in this book to work on this. At some point we were able to communicate to the children our intense desire to have this haven of harmony, and we all began to be aware of our actions and behaviors that aided or detracted from the peace of the home. We also began to hold each other accountable for maintaining the concord between us all.

Preserving the happy atmosphere of the home became a mission for all of us because we found it so blessed to live in such a place. Eventually when someone would argue or speak unkindly to anyone else, the rest of the family would just look at them in disbelief as if to say, "Don't you realize that you just disrupted the harmony?" The guilty person would immediately be sorry that they had been the cause of fouling the lovely mood of our home. We as parents had to be conscious and careful of our actions as well, for when we would interrupt the repose of the home, we would get the same surprised look from our children. It was as if they could not believe that we would upset the delicate serenity that we had worked so hard to build. Of course, it would have been disrespectful for them to have corrected their parents, but their amazed expression was correction enough.

Sometimes we would forget this great truth the Lord had taught us and we would fall back into our old habits for a while. Then someone would say, "Where has the lovely harmony gone?" We would all be back on the same page again and striving to live better. As you work at it consistently, ideas like this will become habits and will weave themselves into the character and fabric of your life. Someday someone will spend some time in your home and they will say, "It always seems so peaceful and safe here. I just feel the Lord when I am here." Your family will all look at each other triumphantly, and in their hearts they will know that, through them, God has built a haven of harmony.

The Constancy of
Communication

✦

Deuteronomy 6:6–7
And these words, which I command thee this day, shall be in thine heart: And thou shalt teach them diligently unto thy children and shalt talk of them when thou sittest in thine house and when thou walkest by the way and when thou liest down and when thou risest up.

Deuteronomy 11:18–22
Therefore shall ye lay up these my words in your heart and in your soul and bind them for a sign upon your hand, that they may be as frontlets between your eyes. And ye shall teach them your children, speaking of them when thou sittest in thine house and when thou walkest by the way, when thou liest down and when thou risest up. And thou shalt write them upon the door posts of thine house and upon thy gates: That your days may be multiplied and the days of your children, in the land which the LORD sware unto your fathers to give them, as the days of heaven upon the earth. For if ye shall diligently keep all these commandments which I command you, to do them, to love the LORD your God, to walk in all his ways and to cleave unto him;

The simple yet profound mode of imparting truth to the next generation as revealed in these two scripture passages has been called the Hebrew Method of education. This form of teaching employed by the Jews required that parents instruct their children at every opportunity within the daily course of life (e.g., sitting in the house, walking by the way, lying down, and rising up). The parent was to constantly communicate to their child the truths of God's Word. In contrast, most of the education in our society today is patterned after the Greek Method. This form of education consisted of an instructor teaching a group of students in a classroom setting. Consequently we have missed out on the blessings of constantly communicating God's truth to our children.

Many parents today spend very little time just talking with their children. There is a fatal lack of communication between children and adults in this culture. No longer is the young man spending great amounts of time outdoors with his father hunting, fishing, gathering, plowing, planting, reaping, and discussing the great mysteries of the universe. It is not nearly as common today for a father and son to spend time on a regular basis just talking. No longer do the young women sit around the fire sewing or knitting with their mother and listening to her expound on the wisdom of the ages. If a family does spend any time together, it is in front of the television where the only people talking are the empty heads on the set. Children today, as a rule, learn life's most important lessons from their peers, Hollywood, or some teen magazine. This ought not to be.

Parents, you need to consciously begin, at whatever age your children are, talking to them constantly about the things that are valuable to you. Share with them your dreams, plans, visions, and values. Discover their dreams, plans, visions, and even fears. Discuss politics, religion, philosophy, history. Talk, talk, talk, communicate, debate, consider together, deliberate together, tell stories, and discuss why you believe what you believe. Talk about life, death, birth. Talk about sex. Talk about sin and its destruction. For goodness sake, whatever else you do, talk to your children. Talk to your sons about good women and bad women. Teach them how to know the difference and what to look for in a wife someday. Talk to your daughters about good men and bad men and about their tricks and their lines. Teach her that together her father and she will find the right man for her to marry. Talk about the joys and the sorrows. Talk about the pitfalls and the stupid mistakes you have made. Talk about your faith and why you believe and how it has affected your life. Tell them about your past and how you want their lives to be better. Let them in on your vision for your family. Talk about it constantly. Talk about the weather. Talk about world affairs. Talk about economics. Involve them in decision making as your counselors, knowing that the father has to make the ultimate decision but they can definitely have input and learn to be involved in the family's affairs. Speak! Talk! Share! Ask! Inquire! Don't let the world fill their heads with its thoughts. Talk about Jesus. Talk about heaven and hell. Talk about the culture and about governments and industries and trivia and anything—only talk.

We only have one shot at this child rearing thing and then they are gone. Pour into them your soul and your mind and your heart. Instead of sitting in front of the television every night, play board games together. Play cards. Spend time together where you can talk while enjoying each other's company. Teach them to share everything with you and to never hide anything from you. Talk. Communicate constantly. Go to war with the world, the flesh, and the devil for the souls and minds of your children. Pursue them. Talk to them. Love on them. Tell them constantly how proud you are of them, how much you love them, what a blessing from heaven they are in your sight, how fortunate they are to be in your family and have you for parents. Speak! Read good books together and discuss them. Listen to preaching and conference tapes together and discuss them. Watch Christian videos together and discuss them and ask questions. Talk about the people you know and explore their lives with your children. Tell them what you are passionate about. Tell them what you would die for and what you live for.

Don't lecture or chide incessantly! Don't nag! Talk. Instruct, share, reprove when necessary, but always talk. Never mind that half the time it will seem that they aren't listening or that they don't care. Don't be fooled. Everything you say is going directly into their little computer minds and they are storing it up for another day when they will care and that information will be needed. Someday you will hear your teenager counseling someone or debating someone, and they will use an illustration that you used with them years before or an argument that you taught them long ago; you will realize that they have soaked up every word and that God has used that Hebrew Method to form and shape and construct your child into the person you have always wanted them to be.

In all of your talking, don't forget to listen. Be a great listener. Start your child talking and then listen intently. When the conversation bogs down, ask some open-ended questions such as, "How did it make you feel when…?" or "What did you think about…?" Keep an open line directly to the heart and soul of your child. Get to know them. Dads should take their sons to breakfast or lunch once in a while and visit with them like a client or business associate. Take your daughters on a date periodically. Mom, take a different child shopping with you each time and maybe stop and get an ice cream cone on the way home and just chat about their lives.

One of the Bullen children's favorite things in the world is to get the whole family in the living room in the evening and have a big discussion. We call it a powwow. We will cover a gambit of subjects. Many times we will recount something we have recently read in a book or heard about in the news. Sometimes we tell jokes and funny stories. We always end up laughing until our sides ache. It is amazing the things we learn about each other and the bonds that are created between us. We are also creating wonderful memories together. Sometimes we play charades or act out movies we have seen. We guarantee you that the scenes played out in our family room some nights are vastly funnier and more entertaining than what is on TV, not to mention more wholesome.

Remember, as you sit in the house, when you walk by the way, when you lie down, and when you rise up, communicate with your child.

The Grandeur of Gallantry

♦

1 Corinthians 16:13–14
Watch ye, stand fast in the faith, quit you like men, be strong. Let all your things be done with charity.

Quit you like men! Be strong! Play the man! Be a man! Cowboy up! Be tough! Stand fast! Do everything with love. This is a beautiful picture of what a godly man is and what we should all want for our sons—that blend of steel and velvet, stone and clay, strength and tenderness that emanates from a young man who knows who he is and whose he is.

Our modern feminist society has attempted to strip our young men of their God-given manhood. They have turned the grandeur of gallantry into an offense. However, God's word has not changed. We must not cower before the feminist onslaught upon our men and our sons. We must stay true to God's word and raise up young men who quit like men (which means they quit when the last drop of blood has left their body), who stand fast in the faith, who are strong, who are not afraid to take on the ideologies of modern philosophy and challenge them from the Word of God. We need young men who are not afraid to be different from the world and who, at the same time, are gentle and loving to children and courteous and chivalric toward ladies.

Recently our family was in a public place and one of our sons opened the door for some ladies who happened to be entering the same building. One of the ladies said with a smile, "Well, chivalry is not dead after all," to which our son replied with a smile, "No, ma'am, unfortunately it is just rare." All of the ladies agreed with a laugh and walked on, having their day brightened just a little. Dads, the reason it has become rare is that we have bought into the lie that chivalry is chauvinism and gallantry is garish. We have, as a whole, neglected to teach our sons the art of being a man.

We need to teach our sons how to properly treat their wives someday by training them to be gentlemen with their mother and sisters now. Our boys open the door for their sisters. They pull back their chairs at the table and offer them their arms when crossing the street. Now that the boys are young men with a business of their own, they will often pay for their sisters' dinner when we go out to a restaurant. Home is a great training ground for gentlemen. Someday our boys will become a picture of Christ as they love, protect, and care for their wives as Christ does the church. They can start now by loving, protecting, and caring for their sisters and mom in like manner. We have taught our boys that they are to be in Dad's stead to protect their sisters when Dad cannot be around. Real men lay down their lives if necessary to protect their women.

We, like King David of old, need to teach our sons to be men of God.

1 Kings 2:1–3: Now the days of David drew nigh that he should die; and he charged Solomon his son, saying, I go the way of all the earth: be thou strong therefore and shew thyself a man; And keep the charge of the LORD thy God, to walk in his ways, to keep his statutes and his commandments and his judgments and his testimonies, as it is written in the law of Moses, that thou mayest prosper in all that thou doest and whithersoever thou turnest thyself:

Some practical ideas for teaching our sons to be men are, first, to have a Bible study with your sons and find out what God has to say about manhood. Start with a study of the ultimate example of godly manhood, our Lord Jesus.

Hebrews 12:2–4: Looking unto Jesus the author and finisher of our faith; who for the joy that was set before him endured the cross, despising the shame and is set down at the right hand of the throne of God. For consider him that endured such contradiction of sinners against himself, lest ye be wearied and faint in your minds. Ye have not yet resisted unto blood, striving against sin.

Second, study men of the Bible. Study the good and the bad and train your sons to incorporate the qualities of the good and reject the traits of the bad in their lives.

Hebrews 11:32–34: And what shall I more say? for the time would fail me to tell of Gedeon and of Barak and of Samson and of Jephthae; of David also and Samuel and of the prophets: Who through faith subdued kingdoms, wrought righteousness, obtained promises, stopped the mouths of lions, Quenched the violence of fire, escaped the edge of the sword, out of weakness were made strong, waxed valiant in fight, turned to flight the armies of the aliens.

These men are vastly more interesting than any comic book superhero, for they were real people, not just the figment of some writer's imagination. As you study the characteristics of godly manhood from the scriptures, consider some of these that we have included below.

- **Diligence and Self-Control**

1 Corinthians 9:25–27: And every man that striveth for the mastery is temperate in all things. Now they do it to obtain a corruptible crown; but we an incorruptible. I therefore so run, not as uncertainly; so fight I, not as one that beateth the air: But I keep under my body and bring it into subjection: lest that by any means, when I have preached to others, I myself should be a castaway.

- **Knowledge and Understanding**

1 Corinthians 14:20: Brethren, be not children in understanding: howbeit in malice be ye children, but in understanding be men.

- **Courage**

2 Samuel 10:12: Be of good courage and let us play the men for our people and for the cities of our God: and the LORD do that which seemeth him good.

1 Chronicles 19:13: Be of good courage and let us behave ourselves valiantly for our people and for the cities of our God: and let the LORD do that which is good in his sight.

Nehemiah 4:14: And I looked and rose up and said unto the nobles and to the rulers and to the rest of the people, Be not ye afraid of them: remember the Lord, which is great and terrible and fight for your brethren, your sons and your daughters, your wives and your houses.

- **Strength**

Deuteronomy 31:6: Be strong and of a good courage, fear not, nor be afraid of them: for the LORD thy God, he it is that doth go with thee; he will not fail thee, nor forsake thee.

Joshua 1:6–9: Be strong and of a good courage: for unto this people shalt thou divide for an inheritance the land, which I sware unto their fathers to give them. Only be thou strong and very courageous, that thou mayest observe to do according to all the law, which Moses my servant commanded thee: turn not from it to the right hand or to the left, that thou mayest prosper whithersoever thou goest. This book of the law shall not depart out of thy mouth; but thou shalt meditate therein day and night, that thou mayest observe to do according to all that is written therein: for then thou shalt make thy way prosperous and then thou shalt have good success. Have not I commanded thee? Be strong and of a good courage; be not afraid, neither be thou dismayed: for the LORD thy God is with thee whithersoever thou goest.

- **Endurance and Single-Mindedness**

2 Timothy 2:3–4: Thou therefore endure hardness, as a good soldier of Jesus Christ. No man that warreth entangleth himself with the affairs of this life; that he may please him who hath chosen him to be a soldier.

- **Spiritually Equipped**

Ephesians 6:10–13: Finally, my brethren, be strong in the Lord and in the power of his might. Put on the whole armour of God, that ye may be able to stand against the wiles of the devil. For we wrestle not against flesh and blood, but against principalities, against powers, against the rulers of the darkness of this world, against spiritual wickedness in high places. Wherefore take unto you the whole armour of God, that ye may be able to withstand in the evil day and having done all, to stand.

Third, read and study good books and materials on Christian manhood with your sons. There are Christian manhood courses that we can teach our sons, such as *Man in Demand* by Wayne J. and Emily Hunter. We can read with our sons such great books on manhood as *What the Bible Says About Being a Man* by Richard Fugate, *The Christian Manhood Manual* by Dave Hyles, *A Man After God's Own Heart* by Jim George, or *The Mark of a Man* by Elisabeth Elliot. One of our all-time favorites was *Raising a Modern Day Knight* by Robert Lewis. There are also some wonderful Web sites from which we have gleaned ideas, books, and articles, such as www.visionforum.com, www.patriarch.com, www.familyministries. com, and www.nogreaterjoy.org.

Fourth, study great men of history with your sons. Read the biographies and writings of great preachers, statesmen, presidents, soldiers, knights, generals, industrialists, inventors, explorers, musicians, artists, athletes, thinkers, philosophers, writers, reformers, revolutionaries, patriots, pioneers, kings, overcomers, orators, poets, world-changers, ancestors, scientists, and so on. Boys have a natural, innate desire to emulate men. Of course, our sons' primary hero should be their dads. This should be trained into them just like anything else, primarily through Mom's consistent edification of Dad to her sons. However, we should also give them genuine heroes like the ones listed above to learn from. If we do not, the world has a ready contingent of sinful, effeminate, undisciplined, self-absorbed, immoral, materialistic, so-called heroes for them to follow.

Fifth, we can acquire and teach our sons the ancient codes and creeds of conduct for gentlemen. There is the Code of Chivalry held to by medieval knights, also called the Old Code, King Arthur's Code, or the Code of the Knights of the Round Table. It highlighted such character traits as courage, defense, faith, franchise, humility, justice, largesse, loyalty, nobility, and prowess.

Interesting are Aristotle's *Nicomachean Ethics*, which include the eleven moral virtues of courage, temperance, liberality, magnificence, magnanimity, honor, gentleness, truthfulness, wittiness, friendliness, and justice.

There is the Code of the West, which was first written about at the turn of the twentieth century by Zane Grey. Its principles included loyalty (riding for the brand), friendship, hospitality, fair play, avoidance of liquor while on duty, generosity (largesse), avoidance of curiosity (not asking too many questions of a personal nature), kindness, the environment (fire danger and protecting water holes), integrity, and religion (the Golden Rule).

The Cowboy Code written by Gene Autry in the 1950s included such ideals as fair play, honesty, trustworthiness, gentleness, racial and religious tolerance, helpful, hardworking, clean (in thought, speech, action, and habits), respectful (of women, parents, and the nation's laws), and patriotic.

There is the Gentlemen's Code of Conduct from William and Mary College, which surfaced around 1736. It addressed three areas of honor and integrity: lying, cheating, and stealing. There is the Lone Ranger's Creed:

I believe:

That to have a friend, a man must be one.

That all men are created equal and that everyone has within himself the power to make this a better world.

That God put the firewood there, but every man must gather and light it himself.

In being prepared physically, mentally, and morally to fight when necessary, for that which is right.

That a man should make the most of what equipment he has.

That "this government of the people, by the people, and for the people" shall live always.

That men should live by the rule of what is best for the greatest number.

That sooner or later, somewhere, somehow, we must settle with the world and make payment for what we have taken.

That all things change but truth and that truth alone lives on forever.

In my Creator, my country, my fellow man.

(As told by actor Clayton Moore, September 10, 1994)

The Scout's Law and Scout's Oath are two more great examples.

Boy Scout Oath

On my honor I will do my best

To do my duty to God and Country and obey the Scout Law;

To help other people at all times;

To keep myself physically strong, mentally awake, and morally straight.

Scout Law:

A Scout is—

Trustworthy

Friendly

Obedient

Brave

Loyal

Courteous

Cheerful

Clean

Helpful

Kind

Thrifty

Reverent

There are many others that are interesting and fun to search out and study. The Internet is a great resource for finding this information. These creeds give our boys an idea of what our ancestors believed a good man was.

Sixth, sons need to spend as much time as possible with daddy. In the world that we live in, it is hard for dads to take their sons to work with them, but we must find a way to spend father/son time with our boys. Boys learn to be men from hanging out with men. When Luke and Levi were growing up, they worked a lot with Dad. From the time they were five and six years old, they would go with Daddy to construction job sites and clean up all the trash, pick up the bent nails, and generally help out.

When Dad was not working, he was on the floor building Lincoln Log houses with the boys or Lego pirate ships. Many days they could be found running through the woods playing G.I. Joe with toy guns and knives. When the boys were older, Dad taught them how to throw a dagger and make it stick. He taught them how to shoot a gun, throw a tomahawk, build a fire, skip a rock on a pond, and a zillion other manly enjoyments. We hiked, climbed, worked, rode horses, went sledding in the snow, made wooden swords and spears, tanned snake skins, hunted rabbits, built miniature railroads, made and flew paper airplanes, and so on. Our boys learned everything they knew about the outdoors from Dad.

Meanwhile Dad was tying heartstrings to his boys so that when they were old they would not depart from his way. Some dads may have different interests than ours, but whatever your interests are, please include your sons as you enjoy them.

Lastly, we must train our sons to be gentlemen just as we would train them to properly throw a baseball. We must teach them the history, importance, and significance of being a Christian gentleman. We must practice with them such things as standing when a lady enters the room, holding the door for a lady, proper speech and manners, and so on. Remind them regularly that they are representing the Lord Jesus in their conduct and conversation. Instill a holy pride for their God-ordained position and calling in this world. Make them into men! An old preacher once told us, "If you will make your son into a man, God can make him into anything he wants to after that."

The Flower of Femininity

✦

Proverbs 31:10
Who can find a virtuous woman? for her price is far above rubies.

The Bible has so much to say about the value of a virtuous woman. It is a fascinating study. Daughters can be an indescribable blessing to a family if they are trained to be biblical, godly young women. As parents of daughters, we have an incredible opportunity to love, raise, and train the wives of future world leaders and the mothers of future men and women of God. It is a high and holy calling. There can be nothing more important, Dad and Mom, than preparing these little girls for their usefulness in the kingdom of Christ. We can see the heart of God in reference to virtuous womanhood:

Proverbs 12:4: *A virtuous woman is a crown to her husband: but she that maketh ashamed is as rottenness in his bones.*

Proverbs 18:22: *Whoso findeth a wife findeth a good thing and obtaineth favour of the LORD.*

Proverbs 19:14: *House and riches are the inheritance of fathers: and a prudent wife is from the LORD.*

Proverbs 31:30: *Favour is deceitful and beauty is vain: but a woman that feareth the LORD, she shall be praised.*

Study the women of the Bible. Teach your daughters about heroes such as Esther, Ruth, Sarah, and Rebekah. Analyze their character qualities and their character weaknesses as well. Instill a desire in your girls to be young ladies from day one. God made them different from boys for a reason. In his all-wise plan, he wanted femininity in the world. Ladies, we must be first to set an example of feminine behavior and habits before our little ones. Next we must diligently instruct and encourage the traits of godly femininity and virtue within our young ladies. Daddies, we must praise and encourage those womanly qualities as we see them in our daughters. Biblically, Dads are to be the primary teachers of children. This includes teaching them about femininity as well. Men, you know a feminine, virtuous woman when you meet one. You know what sets her apart from a loose, brash, or aggressive woman. Lovingly teach these things to your girls. Never be afraid or intimidated to talk to your daughters about the hard things. It is your job! Your wife is your helper in this, of course, but remember Proverbs 17:6: *"Children's children are the crown of old men; and the glory of children are their fathers."* Every little girl has an innate desire to please her daddy. Win the hearts of your girls early and they will hang on your every word later.

In the Old Testament, if a young woman was found not to be a virgin, she was brought to her father's doorstep and executed. He had to look at her bloodstain on the ground every time he entered his home because it was his responsibility to make sure that she was pure (Deuteronomy 22). Fathers, it is our job to raise virtuous young women! The world is running a major campaign to misdirect and misguide our young women from becoming biblical women. It is our job as parents to take a stand and to train them up in the way they should go. Here are some areas of training that we have found vital and some suggestions on ways of instructing your girls in virtuous womanhood.

Feminine and Virtuous Attitudes. We must train our girls to be proud of how God has created them and to learn to think like a woman of God and not as a woman of the world. As we spoke about in the chapter "The Health of the Heart," all the issues of our life proceed from our heart. The first place to start then with our training is the heart. We must teach our daughters the fruit of the Spirit: love, joy, peace, gentleness, goodness, faith, meekness, and temperance. Imagine a young woman who is loving and giving, full of joy and always cheerful, content and at peace, gentle and kind, pure and good, full of faith and love for the Lord, humble and submissive, and self-disciplined and self-controlled. You have just imagined a little girl who is full of the fruit of the Holy Spirit. You have just imagined a virtuous woman. Train your girls to walk in the Spirit and yield their hearts and minds to Christ so that his life shines out through them to the world. When Daddy asks our little girls the question, "What is more important than being beautiful?" they always respond, "Being beautiful on the inside, Daddy," and that is the secret.

Feminine and Virtuous Actions. Of course, once young women have their hearts and attitudes in line, behavior becomes an outpouring of what is on the inside. However, we must teach and train our daughters how to act like ladies. We must teach them Christian manners and what is appropriate for young women professing godliness. Again, the Word of God is our primary source material. Also Titus 2 tells us that we are to get our girls around mature women of God and let them sit at their feet and learn the meaning of godly femininity.

Titus 2:3–5: The aged women likewise, that they be in behaviour as becometh holiness, not false accusers, not given to much wine, teachers of good things; That they may teach the young women to be sober, to love their husbands, to love their children, To be discreet, chaste, keepers at home, good, obedient to their own husbands, that the word of God be not blasphemed.

Our daughters' primary purpose as they grow up is to learn how to be a good wife and mother. That is what they are to be about. They begin by learning to submit to their father and be his helper, just as they will be to their husband someday. They can also be trained for their future role in God's order by loving, serving, and properly responding to their brothers.

Feminine and Virtuous Address. We covered this in the chapter "The Taming of the Tongue," but it bears repeating. We must teach our daughters to keep their tongues from evil and to use their conversation to bring glory to the Lord.

Feminine and Virtuous Appearance. The Bible is clear as to what the attire of a godly woman should be versus the attire of a harlot. Dads, you know what provocative attire on some women looks like. You are the God-ordained protector and leader of your wife and your girls. You determine, from scripture, what is modest dress and you lovingly enforce that in your home. Period. Now on the lighter side, remember that every little girl inwardly wants to please her daddy. If you brag on and make a big fuss over your girl's modest and discreet clothing that you have purchased for her, she will never be tempted to wear anything that disappoints her daddy. If you have crushed that desire to please you by your anger, your negligence, or your untrustworthiness, repent and ask her forgiveness and begin again. Pursue and secure her love. Nevertheless, you are responsible before God to raise virtuous girls.

Feminine and Virtuous Affection. We believe that the greatest training our girls will receive in regard to being a good wife comes from their interaction with Daddy and their brothers. Mom has taught our girls to pour love and affection upon Dad and their brothers. Consequently Daddy and the boys love, respect, provide, and protect our girls as an example of how their husband will be someday. We are a very loving and affectionate family. We hug and kiss on each other all the time. The girls spoil their daddy and serve their brothers with love. When we started talking about writing this book, we asked the children to list all of the things that they loved about our family. The first one that all the girls put down was that they feel loved by Daddy and their brothers and that they always know that we are looking out for them and protecting them. So often a young woman is drawn away from her family and from God by the first young man to come along who pays attention to her and makes her feel special. However, no undesirable young man has a prayer of stealing away the heart of a young woman whose father and/or brothers fill her need for love with virtuous affection.

Here are more practical suggestions that have greatly benefited the Bullen family in raising and training our three girls.

Study the women of the Bible, good and bad, and analyze the character traits that God praised and those that God condemned. Study women of history, good and bad, and see what made them great. Study the wives of great men of history, because the old saying "Behind every great man is a great woman" is usually true. Unfortunately, it was not always his wife. That alone is an enlightening study. As we have said, get your girls to spend time around and sit at the feet of godly women of today, whether personally or through books, tapes, and videos. Find the saintly old grandmothers in your church who exhibit the fruit of the Spirit and find ways for your girls to spend time with them, ask them questions, and learn from their wisdom. Start a weekly, biweekly, or monthly girls' club where mothers and older women teach lessons to the girls on such topics as those we have discussed above as well as domestic skills such as baking, cooking, sewing, needlework, crafts, and so on. Teach girls to be girls. Teach them the qualities of a Proverbs 31 woman. Periodically let them exhibit their talents in music or scripture memory, poetry and verse, or public speaking or readings.

Acquire and read good books on Christian womanhood with your girls. Some of the books that we have enjoyed together are *Created to be His Help Meet* by Debbie Pearl, *The Excellent Wife* by Martha Peace, *Raising Maidens of Virtue* by Stacy McDonald, *Disciplines of a Beautiful Woman* by Anne Ortlund, *Woman the Completer* by Dr. Jack Hyles, *The Five Sins of Christian Women* by Marlene Evans, *Me Obey Him?* by Elizabeth Rice Hanford, and *Beautiful Girlhood* by M. Hale, revised and expanded by Karen Andreola. Most modern Christian girls spend 90 percent of their time learning things that have nothing to do with their ultimate biblical calling of being a wife and mother and the guide of their home. Celebrate and encourage the development of the flower of femininity. Let's give our future generations some Esthers and Ruths and Hannahs to learn from and to be loved by.

The Ecstasy of Enthusiasm

✦

Ecclesiastes 9:10a
Whatsoever thy hand findeth to do, do it with thy might;
Colossians 3:23
And whatsoever ye do, do it heartily, as to the Lord and not unto men;
Deuteronomy 12:7b
…ye shall rejoice in all that ye put your hand unto, ye and your households, wherein the LORD thy God hath blessed thee.
Galatians 4:18
But it is good to be zealously affected always in a good thing, and not only when I am present with you.

The value of being enthusiastic in the work of raising a blessed family cannot be overestimated. The word *enthusiasm* comes from a Greek root that means "God within!" *Webster's Dictionary* defines *enthusiasm* thus:

> Enthusiasm
> ENTHU'SIASM, n. *enthuziazm.* Gr. to infuse a divine spirit, inspired, divine; God.
> Heat of imagination; violent passion or excitement of the mind, in pursuit of some object, inspiring extravagant hope and confidence of success.

Hence the same heat of imagination, chastised by reason or experience, becomes a noble passion, an elevated fancy, a warm imagination, an ardent zeal, that forms sublime ideas and prompts to the ardent pursuit of laudable objects. Such is the enthusiasm of the poet, the orator, the painter, and the sculptor. Such is the enthusiasm of the patriot, the hero, and the Christian.

Our families, lives, marriages, parenting, work, and ministries will flourish if infused with the heat of imagination, passion, excitement, inspiration, hope, and confidence of enthusiasm—literally God within! In Ecclesiastes 9:10, Solomon says in effect, "Whatever you do, do it with passion."

Again, *Webster's* defines *ecstasy* thus:

> Ecstasy
> EC'STASY, n. Gr. to stand.
> Excessive joy; rapture; a degree of delight that arrests the whole mind; as a pleasing ecstasy; the ecstasy of love; joy may rise to ecstasy. Enthusiasm; excessive elevation and absorption of mind; extreme delight.

Can you imagine a husband who is excited about his wife, about their relationship, about where they are going together in life, and about how fortunate he is to have such a treasure? Can you see a man who is passionate about leading his family, who is inspired (spirit within) in his rearing of the children, who is on fire with delight in his pursuit of spiritual and family excellence? Can you imagine how irresistible and attractive that man would be to his bride? Can you imagine a wife who is delighted about the man God gave to her? Can you imagine if she enthusiastically supported him, if she ardently worked beside and encouraged her man? Can you see her zealously loving, teaching, and training her brood? Can you in your wildest dreams fathom how irresistible and attractive that woman would be to her groom? Imagine the impact such a couple of exuberant lovebirds would have on their children and literally everyone with whom they came into contact. Imagine how easy it would be to get the children to love, respect, and admire a mom and dad who were so irresistibly positive in attitude. Can you imagine children who have been trained to find excitement, inspiration, and joy in every experience?

Imagine children who throw themselves unreservedly into their activities, whether school or church or work or fun, and do so with fervor and zeal. Can you envision what a joy and pleasure it would be to raise such kids and how much fun it would be to vacation with them, work beside them, go on adventures with them, or discover new things with them? Are you getting a glimpse of the blessedness of this family? On the other hand, can you imagine the poor child whose parents are negative, sullen, complaining, arguing, and discontent and whose parents drag the child to church and try to tell him that God is good and Jesus came to give him life abundantly and that this child should follow his parents in this faith? This child, the first opportunity he gets, will get as far away from these people as he possibly can, as fast as he possibly can. Sadly he will move away from their God as well, and who could blame him?

Enthusiasm doesn't only have to be something that happens to you when things are going wonderfully. It can be, through practice, developed into a habit of acting. Our personalities and attitudes can be trained and disciplined. We choose how we act. The secret to being enthusiastic is to "act" enthusiastic until you actually begin to feel enthusiastic. The old adage "Fake it 'til you make it" definitely applies here. We must make up our minds, by faith, to obey God and attack life with zest and joy. The feelings will follow as we obey in faith.

We must loose ourselves from the bondage of fear, doubt, and negativity and relish in the blessings of God upon us and delve into life with vigor! In our human frailty, we like to blame our sour natures on personality, circumstances, parents, experiences, bank balance, health, and 50 million other excuses we could probably come up with. However, God clearly commands us in scripture to rejoice and be full of joy.

Deuteronomy 12:12: And ye shall rejoice before the LORD your God, ye and your sons and your daughters and your menservants and your maidservants and the Levite that is within your gates; forasmuch as he hath no part nor inheritance with you.

1Chronicles 16:10: Glory ye in his holy name: let the heart of them rejoice that seek the LORD.

1Chronicles 16:31: Let the heavens be glad and let the earth rejoice: and let men say among the nations, The LORD reigneth.

Psalms 32:11: Be glad in the LORD and rejoice, ye righteous: and shout for joy, all ye that are upright in heart.

Philippians 4:4: Rejoice in the Lord alway: and again I say, Rejoice.

1Thessalonians 5:16: Rejoice evermore.

Psalms 37:4: Delight thyself also in the LORD; and he shall give thee the desires of thine heart.

Psalms 94:19: In the multitude of my thoughts within me thy comforts delight my soul.

According to Galatians 5:22, joy is a fruit of the Spirit of God dwelling within us: *"But the fruit of the Spirit is love, joy, peace, longsuffering, gentleness, goodness, faith."* As we yield to him and by faith determine to be obedient to God's word and act enthusiastic no matter what the circumstances, the Spirit fills us with joy and we suddenly have "God within."

We must also train our children to be enthusiastic. Of course, this starts by us setting the example. Exuberance, after all, is contagious and very pleasurable, so this is one of the easiest things to train into our children and yet one of the most critical to his or her long-term happiness and success. Children naturally emulate and want to be like their mom and dad. They will especially want to copy such a likable and enjoyable trait as enthusiasm.

This quality is also one of the most valuable tools in forming our children's character and gaining their obedience. It is much easier to get a child to do something that they are excited about and inspired to do. So how do we get them enraptured in the things we want them to be excited about? Simple: we act excited about those things and they will follow our lead.

Moms, if we act excited about math, they will get excited about math. If we get excited about cleaning the house and act like it is the greatest thing since sliced bread, they will be excited. How do we get the Bullen children to enjoy each other, eat what we want them to eat, wear what we want them to wear, do what we want them to do? By enthusiasm. Whatever you get excited about and talk happily about, your children will likewise get excited about and embrace. This is huge!

Daughters will gladly wear modest and becoming clothes because they see Daddy get excited about that type of clothing and they see him snub the modern, sensual dress of the world. Their dressing modestly doesn't have to be because Dad has sternly commanded them not to wear worldly clothes, but because they derive such pleasure from seeing Daddy excited about what they wear. What is it that we want our children to embrace and cherish and be enthusiastic about? If we just show delight and passion about those things, our children will clamor to emulate us. Oh! If we could get this truth down into our hearts, it could change our lives, our homes, our churches, and our world. Of all people on the earth, Christians have more to be elated about and to rejoice about.

Sons will want to dress like men, talk like men, act like men, work like men, and so on because their Daddy shows great excitement when they act this way and they are addicted to his enthusiasm in these things. They will love what Daddy loves; they will do what Daddy does; they will even want to look like Daddy, even when they are teenagers, because his enthusiasm is so attractive.

Children will revel in whatever they see Mom revel in. They will get excited about the music, the food, the places, the hobbies, the adventures, and the books that we are excited about. Enthusiasm is incredibly contagious. We should dispense it wherever we go until there is an epidemic of it in our homes and lives! We don't have to be superhuman. We just have to be normal humans filled with God! The Bullen children are so addicted to our enthusiasm that when our daughter came home from her first visit to Christian summer camp a few years ago, we asked her, "How was camp? Did you have a great time?" She smiled and said, "It was great but it would have been a lot more fun if you guys were there.

Those people at camp just don't know how to have fun and get excited about life like you guys do."

Now we are teaching them to become the creators of the enthusiasm themselves so that wherever they go their joy and fervor for life will overflow on everyone around them.

When we lived for seven years with five children in an eleven-hundred-square-foot apartment, we were excited about the little flower boxes on our little balcony and about the neat walkover bridge to the little park with the playground. Our children thought this was the greatest place on earth to live even though it was in a very depressed part of the city because Mom and Dad made it exciting to live there.

Later when we were able to rent a house and get a swing set, we made a huge deal out of it and our children thought we were, of all people, most blessed.

Later when we had to move back into an apartment, we enjoyed the pool and the Dairy Queen was right down the street. Once again, the kids thought this was the greatest ever.

Finally we were able to buy some land out in the mountains, build a little ranch backed up against ten thousand acres of forest, build a gigantic tree house, and have a horse. We enthusiastically plunged into the work and loved and enjoyed every tree and rock.

When God called us to move to Houston and leave our ranch and live in the big city, we made such a big deal out of the tall buildings, the ocean, the new foods, the new and exciting activities, and the new opportunities to serve the Lord that our children loved every minute of it and wouldn't go back now if they could.

Of course, this story is strewn with much failure and we would be lying if we said we were always good at this, but we have experienced in a wonderful way the value of seeing God and his goodness in everything and in always being enthusiastic. We have discovered that whatever Mom and Dad are excited about, the kids naturally are excited about too.

We have talked previously about commanding our family; this is necessary, but the secret to "commanding" a happy and joyful family is enthusiasm. This, of course, works better if we start when they are babies, directing them by our excitement, but even a sour-tempered teenager can't hold out forever against the infectious joy of excitement and exuberance that we can show them, if we will just be steadfast and consistent. Eventually their sullen nature will break down and not be able to stand against a steady onslaught of positive, joyous, happy attitude. Every human heart secretly longs to be filled with joy and a zest for life, but so many times guilt, sin, self-indulgence, and self-absorption have beaten down that desire.

We were married when we were ourselves teenagers. Shortly after, we started a youth outreach in our city called Teens Unlimited. Within eighteen months it had grown to a high day of 1,200 teens purely on enthusiasm, love, the joy of the Lord, and the preaching of the gospel (good news). Over the next few years our family took in over a dozen troubled teens and runaways. Most of them initially had horrible attitudes and attributes, but after a short time of being showered daily with Christ's audacious love, infectious joy, and unabashed optimism, we could see their hard hearts begin to melt and soften. We could see them being drawn wistfully toward our irresistible joy and gladness, and eventually as they were attracted to us they also became open to the claims of the Lord Jesus and his love. We have seen more than one hardened, hate-filled young man and young woman literally break down in tears because we heaped praise and acceptance upon them and acted enthusiastic about having them in our home even though they brought nothing but the stench of a bad attitude with them. Some of these boys and girls are now in ministry around the country with families of their own. God within. Enthusiasm.

The Wonder of Worship

✦

Colossians 3:16
Let the word of Christ dwell in you richly in all wisdom; teaching and admonishing one another in psalms and hymns and spiritual songs, singing with grace in your hearts to the Lord.
Ephesians 5:19
Speaking to yourselves in psalms and hymns and spiritual songs, singing and making melody in your heart to the Lord;

A blessed home is one that is filled continually with the worship of singing. A family that is in the habit of singing spiritual songs together throughout the day will find the atmosphere of their home greatly improved. They will happily discover a growing lack of discord, division, discontentment, and disharmony. There is something wondrous that happens in our hearts and minds when we turn our thoughts to the Lord in song.

The Spirit of God somehow has more of a presence in a home where there is praise and worship happening continually.

Psalms 22:3: *But thou art holy, O thou that inhabitest the praises of Israel.*

There is such a distinct difference in a place where praise and worship dwell that people will walk into our homes and say things like, "I just always feel the Lord here."

David, the sweet psalmist of Israel, about whom God said, *"I have found David the son of Jesse, <u>a man after mine own heart</u>, which shall fulfil all my will"* (Acts 13:22), was not yet a mighty king who had unified Israel and defended the people of God from the heathen; he was a mere shepherd boy who played his harp and sang praises to God all day while watching his father's flock. Remember how when King Saul was troubled in his mind and spirit David would come and play and sing for him and Saul's saturnine spirit would be soothed. In the book of Psalms, David uses the word *praise* 160 times in 132 different verses, the word *praises* twenty-two times in nineteen verses, the word *worship* fifteen times, the word *sing* seventy times in fifty-six verses, and the word *song* forty-five times. Maybe this gives us an idea why God said he was a man after his own heart. May we become more like David.

Sing to the Lord! Sing in the shower! Sing in the car! Sing around the fireplace at night before bed. Sing on hikes in the woods! Sing in the park! Sing in the mall (people will gather around with smiles to listen).

Once, when we were engaged to be married, we went on a mission trip with our church to New York City. All we did for a solid week was stand on street corners in all five boroughs singing songs to the Lord and handing out gospel tracts to the people who stopped to hear us sing. We handed out just over one million tracts in that week. Only eternity will tell the impact our feeble singing and witnessing had on those people.

Sing on the street corner! Sing until you lose your voice! Sing until the tears roll down your face and you remember the goodness of the Lord upon your life! Sing "praise and worship songs," sing "hymns," sing "psalms," but sing. It doesn't matter if you can carry a tune or if you like music—sing anyway. Paul said make melody in your heart to the Lord.

Recently a young man was spending some time with our family. When he went back home, he was humming a praise song, and his mother commented to him how nice it was to hear him singing praises to the Lord. He told her that he had been singing the song in the car with the Bullens, to which she asked, "Oh, do they sing when they are in the car?" His response was, "Mom, those people sing all the time!" When she related the conversation to us, it reinforced to us what a blessing and a life-changing truth worship is and how critical it is to having a blessed family.

Many evenings after dinner, we will all sit around and sing worship songs and hymns. Sometimes one of the girls or Mom will play the piano, and we will all gather around and try to harmonize and find our parts. We can all feel the cares and stresses of the day washing out of our souls as we lift up the Lord.

Let's teach our children to speak to themselves, to one another, and to the Lord constantly in psalms, hymns, and spiritual songs, singing with grace and making melody in our hearts to the Lord.

The Glory of Grace

✦

Ecclesiastes 10:12
The words of a wise man's mouth are gracious; but the lips of a fool will swallow up himself.

Colossians 4:6
Let your speech be alway with grace, seasoned with salt, that ye may know how ye ought to answer every man.

In this chapter, we will not attempt to expound upon the doctrine of God's grace but rather to extol the virtues of families and brethren in Christ being gracious to each other as a result of the effect of God's grace upon us.

The word *grace* used here in Colossians 4:6 is the Greek word *charis*, which is used some 156 times in the New Testament and is translated 130 times as *grace*, six times as *favor*, six times as *thank*, four times as *thanks*, two times as *pleasure*, and one time each as *acceptable, benefit, gift, gracious, joy, thanked, thankworthy,* and *liberality*.

Thayers Greek Definitions defines *charis* thus:

1) grace

    1a) that which affords joy, pleasure, delight, sweetness, charm, loveliness: grace of speech

2) good will, loving-kindness, favour

    2a) of the merciful kindness by which God, exerting his holy influence upon souls, turns them to Christ, keeps, strengthens, increases them in Christian faith, knowledge, affection and kindles them to the exercise of the Christian virtues

3) what is due to grace

    3a) the spiritual condition of one governed by the power of divine grace

3b) the token or proof of grace, benefit

3b1) a gift of grace

3b2) benefit, bounty

4) thanks, (for benefits, services, favours), recompense, reward
Part of Speech: noun feminine

God has shown unspeakable mercy, loving-kindness, and favor upon us, and we should be extremely liberal in sharing that wonderful benefit with those around us. God, who has every right to judge and condemn us, has instead chosen through the sacrifice of his Son to save us, declare us righteous, adopt us, and make us joint heirs with his Son, Jesus. Yet so often, we, who have no right to condemn anyone, go about passing judgment on those around us in a vain effort to pretend that we are holy, that we hate sin, and that we are somehow defending God's honor by excoriating his children. We usually hate other people's sins much more than we hate our own.

We, in some manner, feel more righteous by pointing out the failures of our brethren. Instead, we should spend our energy working on our own hearts and pray for, love on, encourage, and, yes, sometimes rebuke our brethren with all meekness and humility.

Ephesians 4:32: And be ye kind one to another, tenderhearted, forgiving one another, even as God for Christ's sake hath forgiven you.

Jesus knew our natural human propensity for judging and condemning each other, so in the midst of his Sermon on the Mount, he warned us:

Judge not, that ye be not judged. For with what judgment ye judge, ye shall be judged: and with what measure ye mete, it shall be measured to you again. And why beholdest thou the mote that is in thy brother's eye, but considerest not the beam that is in thine own eye? Or how wilt thou say to thy brother, Let me pull out the mote out of thine eye; and, behold, a beam is in thine own eye? Thou hypocrite, first cast out the beam out of thine own eye; and then shalt thou see clearly to cast out the mote out of thy brother's eye. (Matthew 7:1–5)

Again in another place he says,

But love ye your enemies and do good and lend, hoping for nothing again; and your reward shall be great and ye shall be the children of the Highest: for he is kind unto the unthankful and to the evil. Be ye therefore merciful, as your Father also is merciful. Judge not and ye shall not be judged: condemn not and ye shall not be condemned: forgive and ye shall be forgiven. (Luke 6:35–37)

Paul admonished the Christians in Rome to beware of this proclivity for judging our brothers and sisters in the Lord.

Romans 14: *Him that is weak in the faith receive ye, but not to doubtful disputations. For one believeth that he may eat all things: another, who is weak, eateth herbs. Let not him that eateth despise him that eateth not; and let not him which eateth not judge him that eateth: for God hath received him.* **_Who art thou that judgest another man's servant? to his own master he standeth or falleth._** *Yea, he shall be holden up: for God is able to make him stand. One man esteemeth one day above another: another esteemeth every day alike. Let every man be fully persuaded in his own mind. He that regardeth the day, regardeth it unto the Lord; and he that regardeth not the day, to the Lord he doth not regard it. He that eateth, eateth to the Lord, for he giveth God thanks; and he that eateth not, to the Lord he eateth not and giveth God thanks. For none of us liveth to himself and no man dieth to himself. For whether we live, we live unto the Lord; and whether we die, we die unto the Lord: whether we live therefore, or die, we are the Lord's. For to this end Christ both died and rose and revived, that he might be Lord both of the dead and living.* **_But why dost thou judge thy brother? or why dost thou set at nought thy brother? for we shall all stand before the judgment seat of Christ._** *For it is written, As I live, saith the Lord, every knee shall bow to me and every tongue shall confess to God. So then every one of us shall give account of himself to God. Let us not therefore judge one another any more: but judge this rather, that no man put a stumblingblock or an occasion to fall in his brother's way. I know and am persuaded by the Lord Jesus, that there is nothing unclean of itself: but to him that esteemeth any thing to be unclean, to him it is unclean. But if thy brother be grieved with thy meat, now walkest thou not charitably. Destroy not him with thy meat, for whom Christ died. Let not then your good be evil spoken of: For the kingdom of God is not meat and drink; but righteousness and peace and joy in the Holy Ghost. For he that in these things serveth Christ is acceptable to God and approved of men. Let us therefore follow after the things which make for peace and things wherewith one may edify another. For meat destroy not the work of God. All things indeed are pure; but it is evil for that man who eateth with offence. It is good neither to eat flesh, nor to drink wine, nor any thing whereby thy brother stumbleth, or is offended, or is made weak. Hast thou faith? have it to thyself before God. Happy is he that condemneth not himself in that thing which he alloweth. And he that doubteth is damned if he eat, because he eateth not of faith: for whatsoever is not of faith is sin.*

In 2 Corinthians we get a glimpse of the Apostle Paul's heart as he is writing about a brother who had been previously disciplined by the church for a grievous sin.

2 Corinthians 2:5–11: But if any have caused grief, he hath not grieved me, but in part: that I may not overcharge you all. Sufficient to such a man is this punishment, which was inflicted of many. So that contrariwise ye ought rather to forgive him and comfort him, lest perhaps such a one should be swallowed up with overmuch sorrow. Wherefore I beseech you that ye would confirm your love toward him. For to this end also did I write, that I might know the proof of you, whether ye be obedient in all things. To whom ye forgive any thing, I forgive also: for if I forgave any thing, to whom I forgave it, for your sakes forgave I it in the person of Christ; Lest Satan should get an advantage of us: for we are not ignorant of his devices.

James 4:11: Speak not evil one of another, brethren. He that speaketh evil of his brother and judgeth his brother, speaketh evil of the law and judgeth the law: but if thou judge the law, thou art not a doer of the law, but a judge.

We should read the gospels and observe how gently Jesus deals with sinners and yet how harshly he deals with the judgmental religious hypocrites of his day. If we want a glimpse of how God hates hypocrisy, we should read Jesus' caustic and scathing rebuke of the Pharisees in Matthew 23.

God intends for us to be patient and loving with each other even in our failures and shortcomings.

1 Peter 4:8: And above all things have fervent charity among yourselves: for charity shall cover the multitude of sins.

Proverbs 10:12: Hatred stirreth up strifes: but love covereth all sins.

Proverbs 17:9: He that covereth a transgression seeketh love; but he that repeateth a matter separateth very friends.

Of course, we are not saying sin should be allowed in the church or in the family, but our attitude and response to it must be filled with love and mercy. If we err, we must always err on the side of grace. God is able to correct his children just fine. Sometimes he will use us to be part of the correction—his Word makes this clear as well—but as we have said, it should always be with the utmost humility and meekness, bathed in love. Beware of legalism. Beware of Pharisaism.

Galatians 6:1–3: Brethren, if a man be overtaken in a fault, ye which are spiritual, restore such an one in the spirit of meekness; considering thyself, lest thou also be tempted. Bear ye one another's burdens and so fulfil the law of Christ. For if a man think himself to be something, when he is nothing, he deceiveth himself.

One of the reasons that we are not to judge others is that we are simply not qualified. We don't know what is in their hearts or minds; only God does. When we form judgments about them, we are assuming we know their motivations, but there is no way that we can know. We simply don't have all of the facts. God does have all of the facts, and he is infinitely capable of doing all of the judging and condemning that is necessary. He has given us the job of loving. This doesn't mean that love doesn't sometimes have to be tough. It just means that we don't try to do God's job when we are simply not qualified to do so.

Pouring out love and grace on others is like having a checkbook with thousands of checks in it, and as long as you give the money away to others, no matter how many checks you write and no matter how large the amounts are, the checking account always stays full. Would we be stingy with that money? No! Every time we wrote a check and gave it to some needy person, the account would fill back up. What fun that would be! We would be writing checks like crazy! In like manner, God has poured out upon us his matchless love and grace, and the more we lavish it on other people, the more it floods over us. Let's generously shower it upon those around us.

Colossians 3:12–15: *Put on therefore, as the elect of God, holy and beloved, bowels of mercies, kindness, humbleness of mind, meekness, longsuffering; Forbearing one another and forgiving one another, if any man have a quarrel against any: even as Christ forgave you, so also do ye. And above all these things put on charity, which is the bond of perfectness. And let the peace of God rule in your hearts...*

The Sweetness of Servanthood

♦

Matthew 23:11
But he that is greatest among you shall be your servant.

We have talked about "The Health of the Heart" and the importance of training and the discipleship of our children's hearts once we have them in subjection to our authority. Another wonderful lesson in forming our children's hearts and minds to the image of Christ is teaching them to love servanthood. No attribute of our Lord is more amazing to us than that the King of Kings and Lord of Lords, who by his very words spoke 100 billion galaxies into existence, came to earth as a servant.

Philippians 2:4–8: *Look not every man on his own things, but every man also on the things of others. Let this mind be in you, which was also in Christ Jesus: Who, being in the form of God, thought it not robbery to be equal with God: But made himself of no reputation and took upon him the form of a servant and was made in the likeness of men: And being found in fashion as a man, he humbled himself and became obedient unto death, even the death of the cross.*

The most pure and crystal clear image of this truth was exhibited the night Jesus washed the disciples' feet as they finished the Last Supper.

John 13:14–15: *If I then, your Lord and Master, have washed your feet; ye also ought to wash one another's feet. For I have given you an example, that ye should do as I have done to you.*

One of the beauties of servanthood is that not only is the person who is receiving the blessing emotionally healed and changed but so is the person serving. Can you imagine what it would do to your heart to have the Lord of Glory humble himself and wash your feet? We have the opportunity every day to imitate our dear Lord and serve others, making them feel the same way. In the process, we will be changed and conformed to the precious image of Christ!

Galatians 5:13–14: *For, brethren, ye have been called unto liberty; only use not liberty for an occasion to the flesh, but by love serve one another. For all the law is fulfilled in one word, even in this; Thou shalt love thy neighbour as thyself.*

Nothing will transform a child and make him/her more pleasant like serving others will. There is a special blessing of sweetness that comes upon a child who is trained to serve and give. It is the opposite of selfishness, the cause of sour children. The more we focus on ourselves, the more bitter we become; but the more we focus on Jesus and others, the more lovely we become.

Just like training our children to add and subtract, we must train them to be servants. First, of course, we must set the example by serving our wives and husbands and those around us. Remember, more is caught than taught. Our children will do what we do. We can start by teaching them with enthusiasm to serve their siblings and Dad and Mom.

Teach the little girls to serve Dad by bringing him a glass of water or a cup of coffee when he comes in the door from work. Make it an exciting game to serve Daddy.

Teach the little boys to carry in the firewood for Mom or carry (or drag) the laundry basket to the laundry room. Teach them to serve each other. Sometimes have the boys serve dinner and do the cleanup to give the girls a break. Sometimes have the girls rake the leaves and take out the trash as a surprise service to their brothers.

Make serving one another fun. Make it a game. Watch as they are filled with joy at the response they get from the person they have served. Train them to serve at church, to carry packages for adults, to help set up. Look for ways to serve as a family. Take a meal to a family who is ill or has a new baby. Have the children write notes to the visitors from church last Sunday and mail them. As a family, clean the church one week and give a blessing to the janitor.

Be creative. Find ways to serve and train your children to serve and watch God lavish blessedness upon your family. As a family, go help your neighbor repaint his house trim. Help a family move. Get really good at extravagant serving. Train and train and train it into your children until it becomes second nature to them. This is critical to having a blessed family. Think what kind of spouses, sons, daughters, church members, employees, friends, and Christians your children will be when they have learned to be servants!

An old preacher once told us the story of a woman who came to him for counseling because she was going to have a nervous breakdown. He told her, "On Monday, go to the nursing home with some cupcakes and love on the elderly people there. On Tuesday, make some pretty pictures and take them to the kids in the children's cancer ward at the hospital. On Wednesday, go to a young mother's house who has several small children and make them lunch, do the laundry, clean their house, and encourage that young mother. On Thursday, go visit a shut-in from the church and read the Bible to him. Then come back and see me on Friday." The woman was shocked. "I am having a nervous breakdown, don't you understand? I need help here." The pastor smiled and said, "Do this first, or I won't help you. Come back and see me on Friday, and we will work on your nervous breakdown." The next Friday the woman never showed, and when the pastor saw her on Sunday, she was glowing. He asked her, "I didn't see you on Friday, what about your nervous breakdown?" The lady, radiating with joy, responded, "I'm too busy helping all these wonderful people right now. I've had to postpone my nervous breakdown for another time!" This lady had learned the secret of the "Sweetness of Servanthood."

The Magnificence of Ministry

✦

Hebrews 6:10–11
For God is not unrighteous to forget your work and labour of love, which ye have shewed toward his name, in that ye have ministered to the saints and do minister. And we desire that every one of you do shew the same diligence to the full assurance of hope unto the end:

It is important that we realize that there are seasons in a family's life. Initially, when the children are very small, the primary activities of the family will be training, teaching, and molding of character. This will require that the family spend large amounts of time at home working with their children. It has been our experience that this is not the time to go save the world. God may have some exceptions to this general rule, but if we realize how exponentially we can change the world by reaching our children and the next ten generations that they represent, we will realize that our family is our primary ministry in the early years and limit our involvement in outside ministries in this season of the family's life. However, as the children get older and are in subjection to their parents and grounded in the Word, there will come a season where it is time to turn from primarily family building and begin to, as a family, reach out to the body of Christ and ultimately to the world in some form of a family ministry.

As uniquely called and diversely gifted, God will use each family in a different way to edify the body and spread the gospel to the world. The key is that we cast a vision for our children of how God can and will work through our family when we launch out by faith.

As the Lord has moved the Bullen family into the direction of ministering to families, we have been amazed and even overwhelmed at the number of hurting, confused, uninformed, bewildered, and searching families there are in the church, much less in the world. We have found a wonderful and necessary ministry of exporting what God is doing in our family to the families around us, Christian and non-Christian alike.

We know families who are very involved in missions, music ministries, nursing home ministries, family ministries, homeschooling ministries, evangelism, and political activism.

We love to speak as a family at homeschool conferences and give young homeschooling parents hope for the fruit that is to come.

Recently we helped plant a new family-integrated church as a mission of our church. On the way home from church the first Sunday, one of our boys just started weeping because he was so overjoyed at seeing a new church formed and seeing those new families so excited about having a family-strengthening church in their area.

Nothing will solidify in the hearts of our children the truths that we have been pouring into them like the ministry. As we have said, early on in our family, our spiritual focus may be primarily inward and directed at our principal ministry of raising up godly offspring for the Lord (see Malachi 2:15). The secret is that once we have reached that season in our family's life where God has prepared us to serve him, we don't become ingrown and make our family an idol; we take this miniature army that God has used us to create and begin to impact the world for Christ.

Invaluable blessings will develop from our family involvement in ministering to the saints and the lost. We will begin to see the truths that we have been teaching dawn in our children's hearts and minds as they see their practical application through ministry. It will act as paraffin wax, sealing all of the sweet preserves of verity into the mason jar of their souls. It will make all of our schooling come alive, and they will move from the conceptual to reality. As they see God's spirit mightily at work—changing lives, answering prayers, healing homes, and saving souls—their faith will grow exceedingly and their hearts will be cemented in the claims of Christ. We and our children will be drawn together in a tighter bond of faith and awe that cannot be measured and we will be truly blessed.

The Aim of Accountability

✦

Galatians 6:2
Bear ye one another's burdens and so fulfil the law of Christ.

No family is an island unto itself. We are all joined together in the body of Christ. Each family needs to be joined with a local church body so that they can bear each other's burdens and be held accountable by other like-minded Christians. Much is said today about accountability and it is a very biblical concept.

Hebrews 10:25: *Not forsaking the assembling of ourselves together, as the manner of some is; but exhorting one another: and so much the more, as ye see the day approaching.*

Exhorting means to cheer on, urge on, encourage, press on, or challenge. We need each other to stay true to the path that God has for us. Accountability is being transparent with our brothers and sisters in Christ and allowing them to exhort and even perhaps admonish us when necessary. If we genuinely desire for our family to reach its potential for Christ and we are truly seeking holiness, we will be willing to open up our lives and our actions to brothers and sisters in the Lord who we trust have our best interest at heart. Iron sharpens iron, and spending time with other families who are going where we are going and who exhibit the traits that we want in our family will strengthen and sharpen us.

Our first and most important accountability structure will be our family itself. We must instill in our children a sense of responsibility for each other and train them to pray for, watch out for, and hold accountable to the truth each person in the family. In our family, if one of us senses that something seems to be out of joint spiritually with one of our members, we will attempt to pour more love on them than usual and each of us will gently seek to find the source of the problem. We are each concerned about the others' spiritual health, and we are not afraid to check up on each other regularly. Many times we will call what we refer to as a "powwow" and will discuss family issues and challenges, and we will pray

115

together and get things right with each other so that we can again walk blamelessly in love.

Of course, the second most important accountability structure is the church. Seek out a local body where there are like-minded believers with a vision and passion for family and challenge and encourage each other in the Lord. Even in a church that doesn't support the family as it should there are usually two or three families, most likely homeschoolers, who have a vision for multigenerational faithfulness with whom you can form a family accountability group. Have them over for dinner, share your burden and vision of what you are trying to do, and ask them to travel with you in this cause. At different times in our lives we have had a biweekly Sunday afternoon covered dish meal with families like this and have shared, loved, encouraged, and studied God's word together. The benefits have been priceless and eternal. We are currently blessed to fellowship in a family-integrated church called Grace Community Church in Magnolia, Texas, where Matthew serves as an elder. This church has a vision for Acts 2:42–type living and Christianity. We live together in a covenantal community of faith where we share our life, love, help, hurts, and possessions for the glory of Christ. We hold each other accountable and we all agree as part of our covenant to be teachable and transparent with each other. Our church motto is "Discipling Dads Who Disciple Families."

Be salt and light wherever God has placed you. Take the initiative yourself to seek out other like-minded families with whom you can be accountable. Build your own covenantal community within your church or homeschool support group. If God so leads you, start a family-integrated church in your home; when it grows large enough, rent a cafeteria in a nearby school. For more information about planting a family-friendly church, visit www.gracecommunityinfo.org.

The Magnitude of Mentorship

✦

Proverbs 12:15
The way of a fool is right in his own eyes: but he that hearkeneth unto counsel is wise.

Part II of the subject we discussed in "The Aim of Accountability" is mentorship. There is a saying that goes something like this: "Experience is a great teacher, especially if it is some other person's experience." In other words, if we are wise, we will go to the people who have been down the road and made the mistakes already and learn from their experience as opposed to having to learn by making all of the mistakes ourselves.

For this cause, the Bullen family has always been open to learning from anyone who could and would teach us. Furthermore, we have sought out, pursued, and hungrily gathered from those families who were where we wanted to be spiritually. This truth has been an incredible boon to our growth and maturity as a family. We have sought them out at church and sat at their feet. We have invited them to dinner and asked questions and just observed their family in action. We have sought them out at homeschool conventions (we, as husband and wife, haven't missed a homeschool convention since our nineteen-year-old, Luke, was in second grade). We have sought them through their tapes, books, videos, Web sites, magazines, and any material we could get our hands on.

Find godly men and spend time with them. Get them around your sons. Find godly women, Titus 2–type women, and spend time with them. Sit at their feet. Get your daughters around them. Teach your children to observe. Get to know and learn from godly men and women who exhibit the fruit of the Spirit in their lives. Teach your young men how to start a conversation and make friends with good men. Teach them how to ask open-ended questions and get these men talking. Get these men to tell their stories and pour out their wisdom and the truths that God has taught them. Teach your young ladies to do the same with godly women, mothers, and seasoned saints in your midst. As parents, set the example by seeking out wise people and letting them mentor you.

Once when we lived in New Mexico, one of our sons showed interest in computers; we sought out a godly man who loved and worked with computers and who also had a vision for mentorship. This man spent several sessions teaching our son about computer programming and such. The real blessing was that we always knew that if for some reason there was ever a breakdown in the relationship between us and our son and he felt as if he couldn't come to us, he would have Ron and his wife Laura, his mentors, to go to. We see this as a great safety net against rebellion.

Once when our daughters showed an interest in piano and art, God provided Dan and Ruthanne as wonderful mentors who to this day still have a profound effect on our girls. When we worked at helping remodel their house for several weeks, they also mentored our sons and us in many areas. When we needed our sons and daughters to learn hospitality and grace, God provided Brian and Laura as amazing mentors to our children as they would work around their house and get to observe the love of Christ in these people firsthand. There were our neighbors, Mike and Beverly, who were like second parents to our kids and who taught them many valuable things and who showed them love.

Now that we live in Texas, there is a whole body of believers at Grace Community Church who have become second parents to our kids, and it is incredible how God has ministered to our family through these folks. As of this writing, we now have over fifty families that we have adopted as our brothers and sisters at Grace Community. They have become people as dear to us as any blood relative could be.

Once, several ladies in the mountains where we lived formed a literary society for girls called Little Women. Every week they would get together and share their expertise in sewing, cooking, knitting, crocheting, quoting poetry and verse, musical instruments, and so on. What a treasure of wisdom and life application our girls received there.

We currently have a similar girls' meeting once a month called "Beautiful Girlhood" and another called "Women of Virtue." Not only have our children learned many character traits and moral lessons, but they have also benefited from learning construction, auto mechanics, welding, horse care, music, art, computers, landscaping, and a host of other useful skills by spending time with good people, doing good things, and being educated while having fun and being loved.

There are too many families that have mentored us to name them all here, but we must tell you of one example of divine intervention of mentorship in our lives. We were living in a little second-story apartment with five small children in Albuquerque, New Mexico. We had just started homeschooling our oldest, who was seven years old. You can imagine what our life was like with five children who were seven years old and under, two who were in diapers, in a tiny apartment and Lisa trying to homeschool and Matthew working like crazy to keep the proverbial wolves away from the door.

God, in his goodness, moved a family into the apartment directly below us who were veteran homeschoolers. This family—John and Kim, and their three teenagers at the time, Lauren, Matt, and Tina—were everything we dreamed and hoped beyond hope that our family could someday be. They were oozing with the peace of Christ. The teens were polite, intelligent, humble, well-spoken, respectful, very obedient, and obviously in love with each other and their mom and dad. At first we thought that they couldn't be real. Then the most wonderful thing happened. They gently approached us and began to make suggestions about our child training and homeschooling. We soaked it up, and some days Lisa would spend several hours just asking Kim questions and drinking in her wisdom. John taught us much about being a godly father and the spiritual leader of our family, and they all taught us with their lives about harmony and vision and the Lordship of Christ.

We lived there only about six months after they came and then the Lord moved both of our families on, but the impact they made on us will last for all eternity.

It has been said, "The only thing that will change you from the person you are today to the person you could be are the books you read and the people you meet." Seek out wise counsel. Ask, search, read, listen, and apply. Then, when God has formed you into a beautiful, blessed family, return the favor and mentor, share with, and encourage every young family that will listen. Be willing and available, and God will place you around some young, struggling family like the Bullens were in the early 1990s. They need you desperately and they don't even know it, but God knows. Let him use you.

The Cleansing of Confession

✦

James 5:16

Confess your faults one to another and pray one for another, that ye may be healed. The effectual fervent prayer of a righteous man availeth much.

It has been said that "confession is good for the soul," and while not a biblical quote, it is true. Many times we are carrying around guilt that is stealing our joy and giving the accuser of the brethren ammunition with which to shoot us. A simple time of confession within our family can free us of that burden. Many times we have already confessed it to the Lord but we continue to carry it around like a monster on our back. This is especially true of our children. This burden can rob them of the peace and joy that you seek for them. Usually there is something for which they have repented but have not told mom and dad about, and they are afraid of you finding out. This can build a wall between you and your loved one; you won't even understand what is happening and why. Sometimes it is a besetting sin that they have privately fought for some time, and confessing it before their family and getting our support and encouragement will be the thing that they need to conquer it once and for all. Of course, as in anything, wisdom is necessary to decide who hears what. Sisters may not need to hear all that their brothers need to confess to mom and dad or even just dad and vice versa. Mom and dad may not believe it best to confess things to their children that they would confess to each other and so on. Wisdom and judgment are necessary.

We once read a magazine article about a concept called "dead man talk." This father and his sons would set aside times together for dead man talk where they could tell each other their deepest secrets and sins and the others had to respond as a dead man. In other words, they couldn't respond at all no matter how shocking the information was. This kept intimate lines of communication flowing between the father and his sons as well as between the brothers. This way, no one was ever forced to confide in a peer or someone who did not love them and who didn't have their best interest at heart. This caused these sons to trust their father like nothing else could have. It bound them to him with an honesty and transparency that could not be explained. This father would not be one of those fathers who is shocked and saddened later on in life to find out that his son is a drug addict or homosexual or has committed suicide because the son had nowhere to turn in his time of confusion and need.

Once, one of our daughters seemed to be having stomach problems all the time. She would be the happiest little lady for days or weeks, and then her mood would darken and she would complain of stomach pains and discomfort. We sensed that it was perhaps something spiritual but could not discover the cause. Finally, one day something totally unrelated in our home brought up the fact that we needed to have a time of family confession and clear the air over a certain recent lack of brotherly love between our sons. After each poured out his heart about what they perceived was the source of the problem and had confessed and taken responsibility for their sin in the matter, Dad made the statement, "OK, anyone else who wants to confess something and clear their conscience and clear the air, now is the time." Our little girl got up and went upstairs, and when she came back down she had written her confession on a little scrap of paper because she was too ashamed to say it out loud. Dad couldn't read her writing on the little scrap of paper, so they went into the other room and she quietly confessed through copious tears what she perceived to be a very bad thing. Dad brought Mom in, and after they had prayed with her and let her cry it out, she said, "This has been hurting my stomach for a long time because every time someone would mention sin, I would think of this and my stomach would start to hurt." Evidently confession is also good for the stomach! Imagine this little girl carrying around that burden for over a year and the accuser periodically stealing her joy and gladness.

Give your children a chance to unload their burdens so you can help them to leave them at the cross. Help them to understand that our sins are all under the blood of Jesus and that we can walk in victory.

How many men would never fall if they could go to their wife and confess their weakness and their need and have her respond as a dead woman, without getting hurt or defensive, but helping him in love?

How many wives would never fall or turn to another man, whether physically or emotionally, if she could tell her husband anything and have him receive it as a dead man, just listening and then determining to meet her needs and help her work through her challenges?

How many young girls and boys might avoid the shame of losing their purity if they could have gone to their mom or dad and shared their temptations?

How many young people might avoid moral and spiritual destruction if they could have confided in their parents when the tempter pursued them?

Every day, fourteen teens commit suicide in America. How many could be saved if they felt free to talk to their parents about absolutely anything?

When we decide to adopt this idea, we must be prepared to hear some things that will stun us. Sometimes we will uncover things that have lingering consequences, and we will have to deal with those in love and with patience. Sometimes restitution will need to be made or apologies made to affected parties.

However, we must determine in our hearts that no matter what our child confesses to us, we will respond as a dead man every time. If we get angry or hold the information that they have confessed over their heads, we will forever close the door of their heart to us, and the next person they choose to share their problems with may not be the right one. Keep open lines of communication with your child and beware of naïveté. When you sense that something is not right, sit down with them and indulge in some dead man talk. You may just rescue your child from destruction.

The Healing of Humor

✦

Proverbs 17:22
A merry heart doeth good like a medicine: but a broken spirit drieth the bones.

Somehow, many of us have gotten the idea that humor and fun are inventions of Satan and a part of the world. However, God is the creator of humor. He created within our bodies the capacity to laugh and to smile. He created within our brains the ability to recognize and appreciate wit. He put within us his joy and sense of humor. One of the most blessed parts of a happy family is the mixture of love and laughter. Satan only warps and perverts what God has made.

It will be very difficult to convince our children that Christ brings joy and that he came to give us life and that more abundantly if we go around with a scowl on our face all the time. As children of the King of Glory, as heirs of eternal life, we should be the happiest and most jubilant people on the planet. This plays right in with the "Ecstasy of Enthusiasm" that we spoke about earlier. Even if it is not part of our natural personality, we must develop the habit of seeing and enjoying the humor in the things around us. We can bring glory to God by speaking of his wondrous works, by seeing his handiwork in all of creation, by expounding upon his Word, but also by pointing out and enjoying the funny things in life. There is always a fine line between appropriate and inappropriate, and this holds true in humor as well. However, because the world promotes the inappropriate so profusely, we as God's people sometimes flee the other way.

We must learn to laugh, poke fun, tease appropriately, and enjoy the wit that God has put within us. Our family loves good clean jokes, puns, plays on words, playacting, funny accents, real situation comedy (not the lame and immoral stuff on television), and self-deprecating humor. We have literally thousands of "inside jokes" that we are laughing about all the time. We know each other so well that a silly facial expression will tip us off to what another is thinking and we will bust out laughing for no apparent reason. It binds us together and knits our hearts when we share in these hilarious exchanges. We learn humility and to not take ourselves too seriously through self-deprecating humor. This is part of the healing aspect. We can forgive each other and ourselves easier because we have learned to laugh at ourselves and, when appropriate, at each other.

One of the rules in our house is that no one is above teasing. No one is too good to be poked fun at when suitable. Of course, there are boundaries of respect and honor, and all teasing must always be loving and never hurtful. There are powerful bonds and balms that are formed within a family when they laugh at their own mistakes, failures, hurts, and even disappointments.

We believe there is a time to be sober, reverent, and serious, just not very often! Part of the haven of harmony that we spoke of earlier is this concept of having fun together. It is hard to be mad at your best friends. It is hard to hold a grudge against someone who makes you laugh so hard that your milk comes out through your nose. It is hard to be bitter against someone who makes you laugh until your sides hurt and you beg them to stop!

Humor is extremely contagious. Young people who spend time around our family are attracted and drawn because they become addicted to the laughter and the healing that it brings.

The enemy is hard at work to weigh down our souls with accusation, labor, legalism, guilt, morbidity, negativity, worry, misery, depression, judgment, formality, fear, perfection, solemnity, drudgery, and despondency, but these are not the Spirit of Christ! Jesus said his yoke is easy and his burden is light. His spirit brings peace and joy and rejoicing. This is part of what he purchased for us by Grace!

Even the work that we do together will seem easy if we are laughing and joking and playing. Let's make school fun and funny. Let's make learning fun. Let's make working fun. God created within us the desire to seek fun and enjoyment. We must learn to find it in the good things that we do for Jesus.

Dad, stop taking yourself so seriously and learn to loosen up and enjoy life. Learn to collect good jokes. Learn to speak with a funny Scottish, Australian, or Italian accent. Get a pair of Marx Brothers nose and glasses. Be a clown! Why do children love clowns? Why do so many children secretly hate their fathers? Poke fun at yourself. When you mess up, exploit it for the enjoyment and fun of your family. Be real. Be man enough so that you don't have to go around proving it all the time. You will be your family's hero if you will just learn to be silly, playful, and fun to be around. If you can find the balance between family leader and family jester, you can be a larger-than-life superhero. The best commanders are the ones who are so obviously in charge that they never have to say so. Be such a strong man that you can be soft and no one would ever dream of disrespecting you for it.

You can train children to be perfectly obedient, respectful, and loving without the use of anger, fear, or threats. Dads, what kind of a picture are we painting for our children of God the Father? Do we portray him as a big ogre with a club waiting for them to make a mistake so that he can pounce on them because he is so insecure that he needs anger to demonstrate that he is in charge? Are we exhibiting that he is some wishy-washy milquetoast Dad who is afraid to be master and commander of his domain, who sits up there and wrings his hands because he doesn't know what to do with all of his naughty children? Instead, let's depict him as he is, the Master of the Universe who could snuff out our breath with a thought, who is a consuming fire and the one of whom it is said that it is a fearful thing to fall into his hand. Yet he is meek, lowly, gentle, and the most lovable creature in the universe. He has a master plan for each of our lives and he is never frustrated, disappointed, intimidated, or threatened. He is the epitome of strength and he is the epitome of tenderness, all in one.

Moms, if you do nothing else right, be merry. Most other failings can be corrected in time, but an uncheerful mother and wife will destroy a family! Let the Lord fill you with his joy. Submit to him fully in your heart and make yourself available as a spillway of God's joy upon your family. Parents, live as though you were dying. Don't major on the minors. Keep the main thing the main thing. Humor will help you to do this.

It is our belief that good family memories in childhood are a major protection against rebellion in the teen years. Some have explained it as tying strings of fellowship to your child's heart. The more good memories, the more strings of attachment you have tied. Every time we blow up and lose our temper or sin against our family in some way, we cut one of those strings.

Many parents in our society today cut vastly more strings than they ever tie, and by the teen years, they have no strings left with which to reach out and draw their children.

Our family has tied countless strings through humor. We can't count the times we have fallen out of our seats at a restaurant laughing at something funny on the menu. Many times our best memories of a vacation are the funny accidents that happened. Instead of having a nervous breakdown because our plans were foiled, we enjoy the oddities and mishaps more than the perfect parts. When we are 100 years old, we will still be laughing about Dad running over Beverly's foot with the rental car at Mesa Verde because he was in a hurry to make the guided tour. It was intense at the moment, but Mom made it a joke the rest of the vacation and saved the day.

Brooke has a little scar on her upper lip where she fell on her face in Carlsbad Caverns years ago. She cut her upper lip all the way through and so we spent the day in the emergency room. Here was this little four-year-old girl who, when she realized the doctor was going to sew on her with a needle and thread, lifted her 6'1" tall, 220 lb. father off of the floor while he was trying to hold her down for the doctor. We still laugh about that one.

One of the times that we were homeless for a while, all seven of us were living in a little motel room for a month. We made up funny stories about all of the people in the motel, how they might be spies or gangsters or something. We had so much fun, our kids thought we were on vacation.

We are still learning to turn our struggles into adventures. Our family has a tradition of going out to breakfast at a pancake place every Saturday that Dad is not working. Every week we laugh about the time we were in one of these places in Gallup, New Mexico, and it took so long to get our food that we started looking at all of the old people in the restaurant and making up stories about how young they were when they walked into the restaurant. We noticed the chips in the edge of the table and made up stories about the people who sat there before us gnawing on the table because they were so hungry waiting for their food. We laughed until we cried.

We have had more fun getting our vehicle stuck in the mud, broken down, lost, injured, and even a few times when things actually went right! Speaking of broken down, how about the time that Dad accidentally sucked Rebekah's pajamas into the engine of our car and burned it up? That is a story for another time!

We love to read funny stories and laugh until we hurt or read sad stories and cry so that we can laugh about it later. A blessed home is supposed to be a happy place. Be careful about being too intense. Remember, *"A merry heart doeth good like a medicine: but a broken spirit drieth the bones" (Prov. 15:13).*

The Meaning of Maturity

◆

Proverbs 15:20

A wise son maketh a glad father: but a foolish man despiseth his mother.

As we observe families around us, Christian and non-Christian, it appears that many people believe that maturity automatically comes with getting older. They continually exhibit the expectation that maturity is tied to age. However, maturity, which is basically another word for wisdom, self-control, and responsibility, is learned, not automatic. As our children get chronologically older, it does *not* mean that they will inherently get wiser and more mature.

Many of us know of middle-aged men and women who have never grown up. They can't hold a job, don't pick up after themselves, and think that life is about pleasure. These people are children who were never made to mature. They are undisciplined children in a grown-up's body.

Our culture today has set up in our minds certain expectations of how mature someone should be at certain ages. For instance, we don't expect a two-year-old to sit still in church (self-control), but we are angry when our ten-year-old won't sit still in church. We expect them to be more mature simply because they have been alive longer. We have swallowed the hogwash that teens have to sow their wild oats (irresponsibility), but we frown on a forty-year-old who still acts in the same manner. However, maturity is a spiritual quality that is not affected by the passing of time. Our children will get physically and mentally more advanced as they get older, but they will not necessarily get more mature.

Maturity is part of training just like anything else. Reb Bradley of Family Ministries says that maturity is a blend of three character qualities. They are wisdom, responsibility, and self-control. As we train and correct our children following the truths in Proverbs that we have discussed in earlier chapters, God through us will begin to form in our children these attributes. As we lovingly drive out the foolishness, our children will learn *self-control*. As we train them through repetition and correction, our children will learn *responsibility*. As we instruct them and pour the Word of God into them, our children will become *wise*.

To the degree that we are consistent, our children will mature at much earlier ages than is now commonly expected. As we in the Bullen family have learned and applied these truths, our expectation of the level of maturity that can be enjoyed at certain ages has dramatically shifted. We learned when our sons were two and three that they could sit through a church service quietly and respectfully. Usually Daddy was preaching and Mommy was playing the piano, so we trained them at home to sit quietly on our couch with their hands folded and smiles on their faces. It sounds military, we know, but we made a game of it and used praise and enthusiasm as well as correction and discipline to motivate them to obedience. Then, on Sunday, they would sit in the front row, right in front of the pulpit with their hands folded and smiling the whole service. If they started to lose control, Mommy or Daddy just had to catch their eye and give them "that look" and they would snap to again. As you can imagine, all of the adults in that church just raved about and made over those two boys and constantly showered love upon them. The squirming, screaming, fussing, undisciplined, out-of-control children in the church received no such attention. Their parents, through lack of training, were unknowingly depriving their kids of the joy of acceptance and approval that our boys enjoyed.

We now expect our girls to be able to completely run a household by age twelve. No mother of a teenage daughter should ever have to cook, clean, or do laundry again! This is not so the parent can have a break; this is so the young lady will be trained to be a godly wife and mother and to properly run a household.

Doug Phillips of Vision Forum Ministries, in his tape, *The Role of Children in the Meeting of the Church*, explores the fact that in times past, young women were married in their early teens and young men took jobs or apprenticeships or went to sea at ages as young as nine years old. Reb Bradley in his tape, *Bringing Your Children to an Early Maturity*, expounds wonderfully upon this subject as well.

Childhood is training ground to become an adult, not a mystical phase of pleasure and selfish indulgence before the curse of adulthood!

No father of a teenage son should ever have to change the oil, mow the lawn, paint, or do household maintenance again. Train your sons and daughters to be mature. Remember, maturity has relatively little to do with age. Please, don't rob them of the confidence, self-assuredness, positive self-image, and blessing of God that comes with developing maturity at an early age.

The Worth of Working

♦

Proverbs 12:24
The hand of the diligent shall bear rule: but the slothful shall be under tribute.
Without diligence, it is simply impossible to succeed at anything in this life.
Proverbs 10:4: *He becometh poor that dealeth with a slack hand: but the hand of the <u>diligent</u> maketh rich.*
Proverbs 12:27: *The slothful man roasteth not that which he took in hunting: but the substance of a <u>diligent</u> man is precious.*
Proverbs 13:4: *The soul of the sluggard desireth and hath nothing: but the soul of the <u>diligent</u> shall be made fat.*
Proverbs 21:5: *The thoughts of the <u>diligent</u> tend only to plenteousness; but of every one that is hasty only to want.*
Proverbs 22:29: *Seest thou a man <u>diligent</u> in his business? he shall stand before kings; he shall not stand before mean men.*
Proverbs 27:23: *Be thou <u>diligent</u> to know the state of thy flocks and look well to thy herds.*

The absolute best way that our family has ever found to teach diligence is old-fashioned work. Training children to be good workers at whatever they put their hand to will benefit in every area of their lives. Working together as a family is also an amazing bonding tool. As we have spoken of earlier, our culture today sees childhood as a time for play and fun before "real life" sets in and you have to go to work. The Bible recognizes no such phase of a person's life. Children in the Bible worked and played right alongside their parents. It was part of their training and teaching. It is a tragedy that this has been nearly lost in our society today. For the most part, boys in our world today grow up knowing more about video games, television, and pop culture than they do about their God-ordained call to take dominion and provide for a family. Girls in our culture today are more programmed to flirt and primp than they are to become a wife, mother, and nurturer of their family.

There is something supernatural that takes place when a child of any age is given a chance to physically work hard, especially if it is right next to Mom and Dad. Children learn so many wonderful character traits from hard work. We have seen our children learn humility, initiative, tenacity, endurance, courage, self-assurance, and attention to detail. Contrariwise, we have seen children who are catered to and waited upon and never made to sweat or get their hands dirty, who are miserable, lazy, and incompetent. They have no identity, no confidence, because they have never struggled and succeeded.

We read in an article once about a man who said that the way he preserved family unity and maintained a good attitude in his home was by always having a building project going on. His family was always working together. As soon as they finished remodeling one room of their house, they started on another. When they finished that house, they sold it and bought another one to fix up because he saw the miraculous results that hard work wrought in his children. The Bible has a lot to say about work and diligence and also about the slothful person.

Proverbs 6:6–11: Go to the ant, thou sluggard; consider her ways and be wise: Which having no guide, overseer, or ruler, provideth her meat in the summer and gathereth her food in the harvest. How long wilt thou sleep, O sluggard? when wilt thou arise out of thy sleep? Yet a little sleep, a little slumber, a little folding of the hands to sleep: So shall thy poverty come as one that travelleth and thy want as an armed man.

Proverbs 20:4: The sluggard will not plow by reason of the cold; therefore shall he beg in harvest and have nothing.

Proverbs 15:19: The way of the slothful man is as an hedge of thorns: but the way of the righteous is made plain.

Proverbs 18:9: He also that is slothful in his work is brother to him that is a great waster.

Proverbs 19:24: A slothful man hideth his hand in his bosom and will not so much as bring it to his mouth again.

Proverbs 21:25: The desire of the slothful killeth him; for his hands refuse to labour.

Proverbs 22:13: The slothful man saith, There is a lion without, I shall be slain in the streets.

Proverbs 24:30: I went by the field of the slothful and by the vineyard of the man void of understanding;

Proverbs 26:14: As the door turneth upon his hinges, so doth the slothful upon his bed.

Romans 12:11: *Not slothful in business; fervent in spirit; serving the Lord;*
Hebrews 6:12: *That ye be not slothful, but followers of them who through faith and patience inherit the promises.*

Our family has always worked hard together, and consequently an unbreakable bond has formed between us. Also, the work has prepared our children to excel in their adult lives. We have remodeled houses, landscaped our yard, built decks, put in swimming pools, built corrals, and fenced acres of property. On our ranch in New Mexico, we built an awesome tree house for the kids. It had two towers; one was three stories tall and the other two stories tall with a working drawbridge between. It had a two-story twisting slide, swings, monkey bars, a cargo net, a gangplank, a forty-foot-long swinging rope, two porches, secret hatches, and castle battlements. One tower belonged to the girls and the other to the boys. We all worked on it for several weekends, and the kids had as much fun dreaming it up and building it as they had playing in it later. Of course, Rebekah fell from the second story and broke her foot before we were able to finish all of the railings. But that just provided us with something to laugh about the rest of the project. It is always Dad and Mom and all the boys and all the girls right with us working, laughing, joking, and, yes, sometimes yelling and crying together.

We have built many things, but we have also built many memories and built a lot of character into our kids that we couldn't have developed any other way. Often the children didn't necessarily want to help. But Mom and Dad insisted, and later when they saw the results of their labor and felt the pride of accomplishment, they began to catch on to the idea that work is not a curse but a calling. The saying "an idle mind is the devil's workshop" is so true. We need to get our children involved in so much work that they will not have the time to get into evil.

Cut firewood and teach your boys to split and stack it. Teach your girls to cook and clean and do the laundry and knit and sew. Bullen girls can also carry wood and drive nails and build fences and saddle a horse and rake and weed and dig trenches and mow the yard. Bullen boys can cook and clean and do the laundry also.

In our next chapter, we will talk about the profit of play. In everything there is a balance: love and discipline, fun and reverence, and, yes, work and play. Our motto is "We work hard and we play hard," and in both we are obeying.

Deuteronomy 6:6–7: *And these words, which I command thee this day, shall be in thine heart: And thou shalt teach them diligently unto thy children and shalt talk of them when thou sittest in thine house and when thou walkest by the way and when thou liest down and when thou risest up.*

When you work and when you play…

The Profit of Playing

✦

1 Timothy 6:17
Charge them that are rich in this world, that they be not highminded, nor trust in uncertain riches, but in the living God, who giveth us richly all things to enjoy;

Our loving Heavenly Father gives us richly all things to enjoy. He has built us with the capacity to enjoy good things and to appreciate all of his creation. One of the greatest tools that a blessed family has for tying strings of fellowship with each other is their playtimes.

As we have said before, we believe strongly in creating wonderful family memories from which our children can draw when they are tempted by the world to deny their roots and follow the deceiver. Fun and good times are essential to having a well-balanced and happy family.

Gary Smalley once did a survey of 200 families that were close and continued to be close as the children became adults. He asked these families what they thought the most important factors were in becoming a tight-knit family. Of course, there were many different answers including church, family worship, and so on. The amazing thing that he found was that the only activity that was listed by all 200 families without exception was camping. The one thread in his survey that connected all of those families was camping out together and having fun.

We must be careful as parents that we don't get so caught up in our schooling, our work, our ministries, and even our training that we forget to have some balance in our lives. Each family's interests will be different. Each family's financial capabilities will be different. But each family must find the thing that they love to do together and schedule time monthly to do so.

You can only imagine the fun we had with that tree house that we told you about in the previous chapter. In fact, the weekend after we finished it, we had forty people from our church over for a summer party and we had a monster father/child Super Soaker water gun fight. The kids had to defend the tree house

132

and the fathers had to assault it. Every man and child there will fondly remember that day for the rest of their lives.

We have for years tried to take one weekend a month and go on a small road trip to the mountains, some historic site, a festival, a picnic, something! We now live in a city that has professional sports teams that we can follow together. Sometimes we set aside a day to just paint, draw, sing, shop, or watch old movies. We love to hike, explore caves, hunt for Indian arrowheads or pottery, play board games, do skits, and on and on. The key is that we do things together. We are loving and laughing and sharing. We are enjoying God's blessings and his creation. We are enjoying the things that he has so richly given us.

Years ago we made it our goal to visit all of the amusement parks in the United States. Of course, we only made it to a few, but the memories and bonds that we formed on those trips will last until the world has passed away and the sea is no more!

Why should our kids want to be with their friends more than they want to be with Mom and Dad? Our children's friends, though important, could never compete with us when it comes to fun because we are just too good at it. Many times our children have come home from a party or event and said, "It was fun, but it would have been a lot more fun if you had been there. Mom and Dad, you need to teach these people how to have a good time!" Like we have said before, it is hard to rebel against your best friend!

Now, understand. We have never lowered ourselves to the level of our children's peers. Instead, we have raised our children up to the level of our peers. There is a difference! We are not talking about Mom and Dad trying to be a remake of their former teen selves. We are talking about rearing children to a level of maturity at which they become the best friends of their mom and dad.

Of course, with small children, we did things with them that they were interested in. Many times Dad and Mom were seen crawling through the nets and tubes of a playland somewhere. Many times, we were building aircraft models or having indoor water gun fights during the winter and generally being little kids again.

You can be serious all you want at work or when you are dead. When you are at home, be fun to be around. Make your home the place that all the kids want to come to. Become a kid magnet and you will keep your children's hearts and you just might change the world through those kids someday!

The Power of Prayer

✦

Matthew 21:22
And all things, whatsoever ye shall ask in prayer, believing, ye shall receive.

In the pages of this book, we have attempted to share with you some of the wonderful things that God is teaching our family in the hope that these ideas may help your family to enjoy more of what God has for you. However, all that we have said will be for naught if fathers and mothers don't learn to meet with God daily and seek his help and strength to be all that we need to be for our families.

We must not think that in our own strength and wisdom we can build a blessed family that will be the miracle of peace and joy that it should be. We must do business with God. We must pray without ceasing. In the hustle and bustle of our modern world, it is often difficult to make time to get alone with God. But he is always with us. We should be talking to him on our commute in the morning and afternoon. We should be seeking his wisdom and guidance in every area of our lives. We don't have a high priest that is in a tabernacle that we have to travel to. Our high priest is with us at all times. We don't have to follow some religious perception of prayer. We can cry out to him while we are changing diapers or doing the dishes or in the restroom or while we are in bed at night waiting to fall asleep.

Cry out to him to make you the father and husband that you need to be. Cry out to him to make you the mother and wife that you need to be. Seek his face continually. He is a loving Heavenly Father who delights to answer us and help us with our challenges. Ask him daily to pour out his grace, love, joy, peace, patience, gentleness, kindness, humility, faith, and self-control upon you and your spouse and your children. When you are weak, then he is strong. Reach out to Jesus when you are down, when you are tired, when you are weak. By faith reach out to him and see his mighty hand as he works in your family. He has promised! He is faithful! He is capable!

Psalms 10:17: LORD, thou hast heard the desire of the humble: thou wilt prepare their heart, thou wilt cause thine ear to hear:

Psalms 50:15: And call upon me in the day of trouble: I will deliver thee and thou shalt glorify me.

Matthew 7:7–11: Ask and it shall be given you; seek and ye shall find; knock and it shall be opened unto you: For every one that asketh receiveth; and he that seeketh findeth; and to him that knocketh it shall be opened. Or what man is there of you, whom if his son ask bread, will he give him a stone? Or if he ask a fish, will he give him a serpent? If ye then, being evil, know how to give good gifts unto your children, how much more shall your Father which is in heaven give good things to them that ask him?

Do we really believe that we want our children to be godly more than God does? He has promised us over and over again in his Word that if we ask, he will answer, if we seek, he will be found.

Don't believe the Devil's lies that you can't be sure that your family will be blessed and will follow God all of their days. If all we had was Matthew 21:22, it is enough to know that we can have a blessed family. As we discussed earlier, faith is taking God at his Word. It is also resting in the truth that he is sovereign, that he makes all things work together for our good, and that he completely, fully, absolutely, totally, and unreservedly can be trusted. We can rest, by faith, in the fact that God loves us and has our family's best interest at heart. What he has begun and has promised, he will perform!

Philippians 2:13: For it is God which worketh in you both to will and to do of his good pleasure.

Philippians 1:6: Being confident of this very thing, that he which hath begun a good work in you will perform it until the day of Jesus Christ:

One of the greatest faith-building exercises that we ever did as a family was to start a family prayer journal. It was just a spiral notebook in which we wrote down family prayer requests with the date the request was entered and then the date that it was answered. After a few years of looking back in that journal and seeing the miraculous answers to prayer that God had given us, it built our faith to take on bigger and better things for God and to ask abundantly of our Lord. Many of the answers to prayer were quite dramatic, and it cemented in each of us a fresh belief in the power of prayer and God's faithfulness to keep his promises. To God be the glory!

John 14:13, 14 And whatsoever ye shall ask in my name, that will I do, that the Father may be glorified in the Son. If ye shall ask any thing in my name, I will do it.

Epilogue

Rome was not built in a day and neither is a blessed family. Be patient. Take small bites and be persistent. Enjoy the journey. Don't try and pick the fruit too early. Relax. Be diligent but not too intense.

Work a little on your family every day. Study, seek, and learn. Read, listen, question, and seek wise counsel. Soak up everything you can and learn discipline. Keep your vision always before you. Trust God. Lean on him and he will sustain you. Have faith and never despair. Remember,

Philippians 1:6: *Being confident of this very thing, that he which hath begun a good work in you will perform it until the day of Jesus Christ:*

We need to work as if it is all up to us and pray as if it is all up to God. As you launch out in faith and begin to follow God's word in building your family, the Lord will empower you by his Spirit and will exponentially increase the result of your efforts. Also remember that the path to success is many times littered with small failures, but if you're willing to get back up and keep trying, you can't ultimately fail.

Proverbs 24:16: *For a just man falleth seven times, and riseth up again: but the wicked shall fall into mischief.*

Launch out in faith and begin today to construct a family that will bring glory to God for generations and he will direct your path. If you will do this, you will need a twenty-bushel basket to hold all of the blessedness that will be yours!

Bibliography

Ministries and Websites

Listed below are some ministries whose materials we highly value and have read and listened to many things they offer many times over.

Vision Forum Ministries, 4719 Blanco Road, San Antonio, TX 78212, www.visionforum.com

Family Ministries, P.O. Box 1412 Fair Oaks, CA 95628, www. familyministries.com

No Greater Joy Ministries, 1000 Pearl Road Pleasantville, TN 37147, www.nogreaterjoy.org

Patriarch Magazine, P.O. Box 50, Willis, VA 24380, www.patriarch.com

Charity Gospel Tape Ministry, 400 W Main St., Ephrata, PA 17522, 1-800-227-7902

Koinonia House, P.O. Box D, Coeur d' Alene, ID 83816, www.khouse.org

Christian Womanhood, 8400 Burr Street, Crown Point, IN 46307, www. christianwomanhood.org

Home School Legal Defense Association, P.O. Box 3000, Purcellville, VA 20134, www.hslda.com

Books

Below are some books not offered by the ministries above which have also had a profound impact upon our family.

Marriage

Nelson, Tommy. *The Book of Romance.* Nashville: Thomas Nelson Publishers, 1998

Kreidman, Ellen. *Light Her Fire* and *Light His Fire.* www.lightyourfire.com

Womanhood

George, Elizabeth. A Woman After God's Own Heart. Eugene, OR: Harvest House Publishers, 1997

Ortlund, Anne. *Disciplines of a Beautiful Woman.* Waco, TX: Word Books, 1977
Ortlund, Anne. *Disciplines of the Home.* Dallas: Word Publishing, 1990

McDonald, Stacy. *Raising Maidens of Virtue.* Houston: Books on the Path, 2004

Elliot, Elisabeth. *Let Me Be a Woman.* Grand Rapids, MI: Fleming H. Revell, nd

Manhood

Lewis, Robert. *Raising a Modern Day Knight.* Wheaton, IL: Focus on the Family, Tyndale House, 1997

O'Donnell, Michael. *How a Man Prepares His Sons for Life.* Minneapolis, MN: Bethany House Publishers, 1996

Farris, Michael. *How a Man Prepares His Daughters for Life.* Minneapolis, MN: Bethany House Publishers, 1996

Wolgemuth, Robert. *She Calls Me Daddy.* Wheaton, IL: Focus on Family, Tyndale House, 1996

George, Jim. *A Man After God's Own Heart.* Eugene, OR: Harvest House Publishers, 2002

Cole, Edwin Louis. *Maximized Manhood.* Springdale, PA: Whitaker House, 1982

Fugate, Richard. *What the Bible Says About Being a Man.* Citrus Heights, CA: Foundation For Biblical Research, 2002

Elliot, Elisabeth. *The Mark of a Man.* Grand Rapids, MI: Fleming H. Revell, 1981

Farris, Michael. *The Homeschooling Father.* Hamilton, VA: Michael P. Farris, 1992

Homeschooling

Farris, Michael. *The Future of Home Schooling.* Washington, D.C.: Regnery Publishing, Inc., 1997

Waring, Bill and Diana. *Things We Wish We'd Known.* Lynnwood, WA: Emerald Books, 1999

Klicka, Christopher. *The Heart of Homeschooling.* Nashville, TN: Broadman & Holman Publishers, 2002

Fugate, J. Richard. *Successful Homeschooling.* Tempe, AZ: Aletheia, 1990

Fugate, J. Richard. *Will Early Education Ruin Your Child?* Tempe, AZ: Aletheia, 1990
Hamby, Mark. *Education of a Child, The Wisdom of Fenelon 1687.* Waverly, PA: Lamplighter Publishing, 2000

Shackelford, Luanne & White, Susan. *A Survivors Guide to Homeschooling.* Wheaton, IL: Crossway Books, 1988

Child Training

Fugate, J. Richard. *What the Bible Says About Child Training.* 2d ed. Citrus Heights, CA: Foundation For Biblical Research, 1996

Bradley, Reb. *Child Training Tips.* Ex. Ed. Fair Oaks, CA: Family Ministries Publishing, 2002

Pearl, Michael & Debi. *To Train Up A Child (Revised)*. Pleasantville, TN: Michael and Debi Pearl, 1996

978-0-595-37121-1
0-595-37121-3

Printed in the United States
43025LVS00006B/1-102